The Trainer's Toolbox

The Secrets to Creating a Successful Seminar from Scratch

Margit E. Macchia

The Trainer's Toolbox: The Secrets to Creating a Successful Seminar from Scratch

© 2018 Margit E. Macchia
Print ISBN 978-1-949267-04-4
ebook ISBN 978-1-949267-05-1

This publication is designed to provide competent and reliable information regarding the subject matter covered. It is written for educational purposes only. However, it is sold with the understanding that the author and publisher are not engaged in rendering legal, financial, or other professional advice.

STAIRWAY PRESS—APACHE JUNCTION

Cover Design by Guy D. Corp
www.GrafixCorp.com
Edited by: Dr. Karin Hollerbach
Photography: Tara Harris

STAIRWAY≡PRESS

www.StairwayPress.com
1000 West Apache Trail #126
Apache Junction, AZ 88120 USA

Foreword by Margo Majdi

CONGRATULATIONS ON MAKING the decision to invest in yourself by purchasing this book. You might already be an experienced workshop or seminar leader. Maybe you are employed providing trainings for your company; or you might be a total newcomer to this game. Regardless of where you are at this time, the most important thing is—you are here and are getting ready for the adventure of a lifetime.

The Trainer's Toolbox, written by my former student Margit Macchia, delivers an outstanding workbook that anyone can easily use to get all the information needed to create world class workshops and seminars that any trainer can be proud of.

The book is filled with the know-how and step-by-step instructions to become successful as a workshop leader, trainer or seminar leader or to build on a trainer's existing expertise to deliver even more powerful programs to their participants. *The Trainer's Toolbox* is well organized and written in such a manner that it can be used again and again to look up things you might have forgotten over time.

Margit masterfully goes into details on how, when, where, and what is important during the process of creating a program or a performance. Every page in this book is laced with humor and a no-nonsense writing style, but mostly with proven facts that she learned by observing and trying things out herself and by watching many international trainers.

Once you are clear about your topic, there is nothing to stop you from your goal of becoming a trainer yourself and leading a powerful workshop or seminar. Every detail is covered from where to find your venue and how to negotiate it, to how to set up your chairs, control the temperature in the room, and why you want to keep the doors and windows closed while the seminar is going on.

Margit covers who you have to be as a trainer to get your message across to your participants with excitement and fun. She gives you an outline and an explanation of how to create your presentation that will establish you as a successful trainer and bring you closer to financial wealth.

Many people are inspired to become workshop leaders or trainers because they want to support participants solve their problems. But they shy away from the endorsement of their products and therefore forgo the revenue they could acquire.

Margit teaches and explains to you the power of providing an irresistible offer that will inspire participants to purchase your products or follow-up programs.

Last but not least Margit also reveals the ten biggest mistakes seminar leaders can make and how to avoid them.

Margit is an extraordinary woman of principle and vision, who takes life and her capacity of bringing out the best in people. Knowing how impactful her insights are of people, she wrote this book with passion, to make the experience of being a trainer something to aspire to.

As an owner and CEO of Mastery in Transformational Training and having had the opportunity to get to know Margit as one of my students in the year 2002, I feel privileged to write these words with the hope that you, too, will create extraordinary results from the knowledge given to you in *The Trainer's Toolbox*.

—Sincerely, Margo Majdi
President and CEO of Mastery in Transformational Training
President and founder of the Torch Foundation Training
Author of *The Art Of Acknowledgment* and *Workshop of Art of Acknowledgement*

Table of Contents

Who is Margit and Why Did She write this Book?

AS PART OF Margit's past work experience, she worked as a business coach with one of the largest, most successful, international educational seminar companies. Margit also brings hundreds of hours of volunteer time to *The Trainer's Toolbox*.

She was lucky enough to have had the opportunity to work directly with the masters of seminar leaders and the best of the best of production crews.

Margit participated, volunteered and worked in seminars with companies like Landmark Education, Mastery in Transformational Training, Peak Potentials, New Peaks, Magnetize your Audience, Celebrating Men/Satisfying Women, and Mindset System for Success.

She not only spent time in the chair as a participant, but you could say she has done it all. From working at the check-in desk, to welcoming participants, setting up thousands of chairs (she is not kidding), handling payments, troubleshooting when things did not go the "right" way, running the handouts and microphones, coaching participants, managing the volunteer team, assisting the technical crew, being the personal assistant to "the" seminar leaders, and finally graduating to being on stage herself.

Margit also has over twenty years of marketing experience,

twenty years of planning and managing fundraising events, and over twenty thousand hours of coaching international clients on five continents.

For the past six years, she spent time on stages in Italy, Austria and the USA, leading business seminars and training the trainers. With her successful toolbox of knowledge, she would love to help you, the reader, create outstanding seminars and/or workshops that rock the world of your participants, so they keep coming back for more.

Her intention is to show you, how you can make great money by doing what you love to do—i.e. sharing your knowledge through leading seminars—creating financial success for yourself and your family in an effective and proven way.

But before she does that, she will tell you a short story.

From the mouth of Margit

In the past year I had the opportunity to lead another successful (sold out) seminar in Austria. Our participants learned how they can create and teach their individualized seminars, sharing their expertise, and loving it all the way. In a very simple way (almost too simple—because I teach a system that can't fail)—you too will learn how to dip into the toolbox and the system.

I'm sad to say, it was not always that way. In 2007, I had just become Featured Photographer of the Year at the Los Angeles Photography Convention. Over 100 people sat in the auditorium waiting for an hour-long presentation on how they too could have a great photography business. Everyone wanted to hear how this woman (me) was able to create a successful business in such a short time.

To keep this story short, within the first twenty minutes, half the participants left, and the rest were utterly disappointed. I was devastated, trying to hold back tears; my voice was shaky, and I was looking for a way out. Though I worked very hard at preparing my seminar, it was a huge flop.

Today I know it wasn't that I didn't have great information for the participants, I just didn't have the knowledge (i.e., tools) to captivate the audience. Neither did I know how to teach or inspire anyone in the room. I had no understanding of the problems these participants were facing. It was a far cry from me having any fun or entertaining the participants. There was no possibility at all of selling programs to generate future income.

In the middle of the presentation, when people started to leave, by the grace of God, a good friend of mine saved me by taking over the seminar. Not surprisingly, after that, I never went back to that convention, and I gave up my photography business for good—I never wanted to give any kind of speech, workshop, or seminar again (or even open my mouth in front of anyone near or on a stage).

My photography career and my stage career were over for good. There was no way I ever could face my colleagues again, or so I thought. It took me almost six years and hundreds of hours of being surrounded by the masters of seminar leaders, until I once again had the courage to set foot on a stage. But, this time I was armed with "The Trainer's Toolbox", the knowledge and the knowhow in my back pocket.

The rest is history, as they say. Now I am eager to share my knowledge with people like you, so you never have to live through an experience like I had on that devastating day.

I know with this book, "The Trainer's Toolbox" and a little practice and planning, giving a seminar will be easy for you—because it really is with the right tools, the right knowledge and the right you.

If I can do it, so can you!

So, let's begin.

Why the World Needs You. Yes, YOU!

You were born to win. But to be a winner, you must plan to win, prepare to win, and expect to win.
—Zig Ziglar

The world needs you and people like you because you have a gift, a passion or a natural talent for something. Some of us have certain knowledge or have learned a special skill; some of us are even born with it. No matter how we got there, we all have something to offer—and we all have a duty to share it with others.

None of us are born to be perfect seminar or workshop leaders or trainers; but all of us can learn and maximize the opportunity to share our knowledge, inspire others, make money with our gifts and talents, and do what we are meant to do in this lifetime: live life to the fullest and to have joy, fun and happiness as part of our financial success.

The problem is that we think we are not good enough or talented enough. We think that this knowledge or gift we have, everyone else has too, and we believe, therefore, that no one needs it in the first place. You are wrong!

Just as everyone has a book in him/her, so everyone can be a successful trainer, workshop or seminar leader in his or her own field of expertise. With this book I would like to show you how. All you need are these tools and a little confidence (a little confidence equals being in action) and off you will go to you leading your very own special seminar!

For simplicity, I will from now on use presentation or seminar or workshop leader, or trainer (but not all at once!), as appropriate in the sentence, and I will use either he or she to refer to people of any gender.

The Trainer's Toolbox

The two most important days in your life are the day you are born and the day you find out why.
—Mark Twain

You do not necessarily need to be an experienced trainer to benefit from this book. You can be a hairdresser, teacher, doctor, attorney, real estate agent, plumber, etc. and yes, you too can lead inspiring workshops. If you have clients that need to be educated about what you are doing or if you want to attract more clients in to your business world—this book is for you.

With short seminars you can win the trust of your potential clients within an hour by showing them how you can help them with your knowledge or your products.

You let them know that you understand their problem or pain; and you let them know that you are the solution to getting their problem solved.

You have a great business when you understand the pain of your customers and you have found a way to ease or solve that pain for good.

Becoming an awesome trainer also gives you the opportunity to present a sale (notice I didn't say you sell them something). You give them the opportunity to experience an irresistible offer for them to choose to purchase your products. Your clients will want to do business with you!

Giving a presentation to your existing clients or your future potential clients is one of the least expensive marketing tools out there. You simply invite people and give them an hour of attention. They walk away happy, satisfied and educated about you and what you have to offer.

On top of that, they'll have just purchased your products—and that means money in your pocket.

One of my clients in Austria has shared with me:

You know Margit, my customers are really happy with my services, but when I ask them to refer me to their friends and family, it just doesn't happen.

I told him that most of his clients probably don't really know how to properly refer him. Sometimes it is hard for people to express in words what you actually do for them. They just know that you solved their problem.

A mini workshop is the perfect opportunity to solve the problem of helping your clients learn how to refer you to their friends and family. They can even bring their friends and family to your presentation and let them find out right there why they, too, should be coming to you, using your services or products.

Either way, you will get more business through referrals and happy customers. So don't wait—make the decision now to become a great trainer/presenter and market yourself as well as your products successfully.

I will show you how in this book.

Start where you are. Use what you have. Do what you can.
—Arthur Ashe

Toolbox 1—Stuff You Need to Know Before You Start

To me, business isn't about wearing suits or pleasing stock-holders. It's about being true to yourself, your ideas and focusing on the essentials.
—Richard Branson

Who is Your Perfect Participant?

THE PERFECT PARTICIPANT is the person that has a problem that you can and are willing to solve for him. The bigger the issue, the better a client he or she will be for you. The issues can be in several areas of life.

I'd like to mention the top five where people are willing to spend their time and money to get help: relationships, health, spiritual growth, financial (money, business, financial growth) and sex. The bigger the issue, problem or pain, the more willing your clients are to receive advice or help from you.

Here are ten important points to consider when evaluating your ideal seminar participant:

1. Are your ideal participants male or female? I would have

quite a different presentation for only male or only female participants, or when both are present.

2. What are the three biggest issues your potential participant is experiencing, and can you solve one or all of these issues?

3. If you give seminars for children under the age of 18, beware, they are not your ideal participants—their parents are! The parents are the ones that usually pay for the seminar. There are exceptions, but they are rare.

4. Is your potential participant financially well off? Presentations to broke people don't create income for you—your ideal participant is able to afford your products and services. That does not mean that once you are established you can't give away scholarships and help people in need.

5. Does your participant want to invest in the service that you provide? Some might need it, but may not be willing to pay for it.

6. Where does your ideal participant live? If not local, you must ask yourself, is she willing to travel? Many are—if there is a huge value and importance for them in the seminar. If not, it will be a challenge for you.

7. Participants must believe that you can solve their issues, and they must see value in your seminar.

8. If you want participants to come to your seminar for more than a few hours, it usually helps if they've had a chance to experience you beforehand (that is where the 60 and 90 minute presentations come into play).

9. Participants must be willing to give you their time and open their wallets. Time and money are forms of payment. Some might have the money, but don't want to give you the time, or vice versa. Both must be given willingly.

10. Just because you believe you have a great product or service, doesn't mean your participants know that. Prove it to them!

Don't find customers for your products, find products for your customers.
—Seth Godin

What Do Your Participants Want to Learn from You?

The answer is simple, they want to learn how to solve their problems or at least ease their pain. When they sit in your presentation they are going to ask themselves, "What's in it for me?" and you'd better have a great answer. You must know and understand their biggest problems (in your field of expertise) and be able to communicate to them that they are in the right place to solve these issues. Help is on the way!

Knowing and understanding, as well as being able to solve their problems, will be a great help when you go out to market to your ideal clients. Even though you will learn a few things about marketing, this book is not about that. Today, we'll just focus on *The Trainer's Toolbox* so you can create and deliver an amazing seminar, workshop or training.

How do you Pick the Perfect Venue?

Your perfect venue depends on how many participants you anticipate. Is it a small group of 20 to 50? Or is it a hundred participants or even a thousand or more? I have worked with all sizes of groups, on and off stage, and the rules are the same—pretty much.

The most important ones are that in your presentation, while it is going on, the participants are not disturbed by outside noise, bad smells, open windows and doors, or intruders. Make sure the venue has a certain ambiance, parking is convenient, and the facilities are easy to find and to access. Plenty of clean bathrooms are a big plus, and it is always good to have restaurants nearby.

Make sure that you have a place for a stage, chairs for the participants and a sales table. How the room is set up, I'll cover in a later chapter. Keep reading, and by the end of the book you will be clear on what you need for the size of participants you are going to have.

Room Prices are Always Negotiable

Seminar rooms can be frightfully expensive—we want to consider this before we start to negotiate with the sales manager. The hotel has the right to make money, and they should. But especially at the beginning of your seminar career you don't have a lot of extra cash laying around to give to the hotel manager.

Nevertheless, it is important to have nice rooms available for your participants. How can you save money and have great value at the same time, with a great venue of your choice? Negotiate—enroll the hotel manager into your project and figure out what's in it for her.

About 100 people or more will be visiting her venue (great marketing for the hotel); they will be eating here (great weekend, or weekday business); etc. You also can reserve a certain number of rooms that you will guarantee and then offer to your participants for a special price. Most hotels will give you a special rate for your participants, the more, the better. This way, many times you not only negotiate the seminar room price down, you may also end up getting your own personal room for free, which helps tremendously with your budget. You know what I mean.

To negotiate the price of the seminar room it helps to find out when it is the venue's off-season. Usually those are the best times for reasonable prices, and for availability.

Don't assume that the hotel manager or owner will say no. It never hurts to ask. If one venue won't give you a great deal, try another one—you will find the right one for the right price at the right time. You'll get the hang of it!

Not Every Stage is Created Equal—Create a Space that Works for You

Your stage should be about one to two feet higher than the participants' level, and it should be about six feet away from the first row, depending how large the room is. Please make sure that the first row is not too close to the stage. I usually get on stage before the event and just know what the right distance is—it feels right to me. So make sure it feels right for you!

You might say: "I don't need a stage", or "I don't have enough participants in my course to justify a stage." It's your choice, but think about it. It is your responsibility to ensure that your participants can see and hear you with ease. They also need to be able to see your flip chart, as well as your props, without having to twist their necks looking around other people's heads to get a glimpse of you. If you don't have theatre elevation where the participants sit, it will be a challenge to get the full experience without distractions for anyone sitting beyond the third row.

So what should be placed on the stage? Standing on the stage, looking at the participants, I have a table on the right, which is covered with a tablecloth to the floor. One should never see the feet of the table or worse, what is stashed below the table. It is a great place to put your personal belongings if you don't have an extra room dedicated to you during the seminar, as long as everything is out of sight from your participants.

It is also a great place to store extra giveaways, an extra pair of shoes, your purse, etc.

On the table there should be a beautiful flower arrangement. Make it your personal space of beauty. It is totally okay also for men. Flowers won't diminish your masculinity, not at all.

What you need on the table is a glass of water (with lemon and/or honey to keep your voice healthy). I like a nice wine glass—but make sure you don't accidentally spill anything. A closed water container might be preferable. I also like tea with honey/lemon in a cup and saucer. No coffee with milk—it is not good for your voice. In case your voice has not yet been trained by a speech coach, you might also want some throat lozenges that you can take quickly—but make sure they are unwrapped, so you don't have to fuss with the crackly paper. Never speak into the microphone while you are chewing candy, gum, or anything else for that matter.

Please, no food on that table. You never want to eat in front of your participants while you are on stage, unless it is a cooking show.

Giveaway stuff—you might want to give away some prizes like T-shirts, books, CDs—free stuff to have some fun with your participants.

Note—I usually place my notes on a music stand that might be either in the middle of the stage or in front of the director's chair (where I will sit while my participants work by themselves or in groups). I do not recommend a podium for notes, because it creates a personal divider between you and your participants. The music stand is small, light and movable, and not as obvious.

Pens—I like to take notes of ideas or feedback during the seminars to improve future seminars.

Props—I use them to visually inspire participants or to get across key points in what I'm teaching.

On the left side of me I have a flip chart; either it has a place to put the markers on the flip chart, or I have a small chair or table right next to it, for a basket with lots of markers.

Lots of markers—just in case one runs out or is dried up (oops…I forgot to close them properly on the previous day). Don't ever use old markers that don't work—it's best to try them out before the seminar.

Some people use more the one flip chart—that is okay too.

There is a possibility that you may have feedback from the speakers on stage or from prompters. Make sure nothing gets in the way of creating a connection between your participants and you.

Another very important part that relates to being on stage and having a good stage presence: never allow your participants to walk on stage from the front. Always invite them to walk up some stairs on the side. You yourself should also never go or jump on stage from the front, unless you are singing with a rock band and that is part of the show.

This is a little thing, but as a professional seminar leader, always walk up from the left or right side unto the stage, and never jump.

What Should be behind the Stage and under the Table

Always bring a second pair of shoes—heels have been broken off on the stage.

Beyond that, from my own experience, I can't walk all day long in the same pair of shoes. Please also stay away from high heels, flip-flops or open shoes that easily slip off.

Make sure you have extra clothing (skirts, shirts, pants, stockings) handy. You won't have enough time to replace buttons or to wash out something that spilled on you. Changing your blouse or shirt is just easier and faster. People that sweat a lot should consider changing during lunch or dinnertime at least once.

Women, remember to bring extra tampons, make-up, lipstick and the like—but never put lipstick on when on stage and in front of people.

Everyone, bring a toothbrush, hairbrush, snacks and water—whatever you can think of.

I also like baby wipes to wipe my hands if I can't get the chance to wash my hands. Those are little things that will make your life on stage less hectic…I promise.

I am assuming most speakers have a room rented where all of these things can be kept, but if your room is too far away from your seminar room, or you don't yet have a personal assistant who can keep all that stuff for you, you must have it handy for yourself.

Flip Chart versus PowerPoint—Could Technology Get in Your Way?

Even though Microsoft PowerPoint (or other slide) presentations formats can be in many ways more creative and for sure more eye-catching, they also come with a lot of limitations I'd like to mention here, so please don't fight me on using a flip chart—especially if you are just starting out and are organizing small intimate seminars (between 10 and 50 people). Of course, always try out both and then decide what works best for you.

Here are a few things you have to consider.

When you use PowerPoint, most of the time you have to dim the lights in the room, even just a little, for better visibility. And what just happened? You just lost James—he is fast asleep in the last row. Even if he's not, instead of being focused on you, he is focused on the words that are written on the screen. Yes, he is reading every word and syllable—you just helped him direct his focus where you don't want it to be.

What happens if the technology breaks down? Will you be able to smoothly continue your seminar or should we send the participants home for the day? Also, digital text doesn't have the same impact as handwritten text on flip charts, so keep reading—this information can make or break your seminar. Last but not least, if you really have to use PowerPoint, then please mostly use photos, drawings or cartoons with a splash of a word or two, here and there.

Under no circumstances write your entire curriculum on the screen so that participants can read it, before you can talk about it.

Why?

Because you just lost their undivided attention.

Also consider whether you are trying to wing it in the seminar, i.e. you don't really know your stuff or maybe you are just using the presentation as a crutch? I know for myself, I used to love using PowerPoint because I was so worried that I would lose my place, or lose my train of thought and forget my words. That used to be my biggest fear, even though it never actually happened. Being a seminar leader can be a nerve-wracking occupation at times until you learn to totally enjoy yourself and to accept that mistakes happen—and that mistakes are okay.

I'd also like to share with you that using notes is completely acceptable. That is my opinion and the opinion of most world-class speakers. I know, because I have asked them many times. After all, we all got started somewhere. Some speakers still use a music stand or work with a prompter. There are of course some exceptions, like those in Anthony Robbins' league. I am not on that level of seminar leader, but it doesn't matter. Maybe one day I will be, and until then I am comfortable using whatever I need to create and present an awesome seminar.

Now let's get to the flip chart and why I am so in favor of it. Let's talk about how to use it correctly to have a lasting impact on your participants.

With a flip chart you can create curiosity, anticipation and suspense; and you entertain your participants. Let me give you a hint:

> *Always stand in front of the flip chart when you write something down. Never stand on the side and let them see what you are writing. In general, people are curious and want to know what you are doing. This keeps the suspense and therefore the*

anticipation high—you got their attention and that is exactly what you want to have from your participants. At the same time that you are delivering your important message, you are entertaining them. As a result, they will learn faster and better.

Here are seven flip-chart rules that will make a big difference:

Never pre-draw or pre-write your flip chart.

Use BIG, FAT markers.

Use at least two or more colors (three or four are best).

Use the entire surface of the page.

Stand in front of the flip chart when writing.

Write in large, clear letters.

Repeat what is written on the flip chart either yourself or allow your participants to read it out loud, either as a group or as individuals.

Never pre-draw or pre-write on the flip chart, because you don't want participants to read what is written before you talk about it. As you stand in front of the flip chart, while you are writing or drawing what you want to communicate to your participants, you create suspense. People will wonder what you have to reveal that is so important, and that helps you keep the seminar interesting.

Why BIG, FAT markers?

Keep in mind that many people are not sitting in the front row. Participants in the back also want to be able to read what you have written on the paper. Why two or more colors? Again, to keep your information visually interesting and easier to read.

Once I saw a seminar leader writing clearly but in very small letters. I couldn't have read his text even if I had been standing next to the flip chart. Some seminar leaders want to save paper and write a lot of information on one sheet of paper—big mistake! Always use up the entire surface of the paper and use a lot of paper.

Why?

On your next break you will be hanging the flip chart papers on the walls. That's assuming it's a one-day seminar. If it is longer than one day, I usually wait until the evening when everyone has gone home or to their hotel rooms. Do it when the day is done, but definitely before the next morning.

The next day, in the morning before you get started with the new day's curriculum, allow your participants some time to review each flip chart in teams of two or three. This is part of the accelerated learning tools. Repeating what one has learned within a short period of time after learning it will help participants remember more and for the memory to last longer.

You also can use the flip chart as a tool to interact with your participants. Allowing participants to come on stage and become helpers that write things down lets you keep the focus on your material.

Have fun with it!

With the help of the flip chart you will convey to your participants that you are having fun and the message you are delivering to them will stick in their memory.

Microphone—a Tool You Don't Want to Do Without

Many times beginners tell me they don't need a microphone: "I only have twenty people in the room and they can hear me loud and clear."

The only thing I can tell you: invest in a good microphone system and use it. Now I know you don't trust me yet, so I will give you several reasons.

- You will save your voice. It is much easier to speak in a normal tone of voice than to yell so the last row can hear you.

- It is a tool to assist you in controlling the energy in the room effectively and without abusing your voice. Sometimes a whisper is more effective than yelling.

- You can use the microphone to modulate your voice—speaking softly or loudly, whispering, speaking clearly or powerfully and the voice itself becomes a great communication tool.

- It not only looks professional—you feel like a professional!

Set up Your Room for Success—Arranging Chairs to Promote Learning and Avoid Distraction

Your job as a trainer is to control the energy in your room. You might read this more than once in this book, but the bottom line is: if you don't control the energy in the room, then your participants will. In that case, you might or might not have a successful seminar outcome. Setting up your room is a very important part of your seminar—nothing is left to chance.

One of the most important aspects of this is the seating arrangement. The set-up will make all the difference—it will determine whether your participants will or will not pay attention to what you are saying. It should be a space where learning becomes a pleasure and comfortable, but not too comfortable.

There are four basic different styles of setting up your chairs:

- U-shape

- Boardroom

- Classroom

- Theatre Style

… and here is my opinion on them.

Even though I will only use the theatre style in my seminars (except with Mastermind Groups) I'd still like to explain the pros and cons of all four styles.

U-Shape: The tables are set up just like it says in a "U-shape", and the chairs are placed on the perimeter. That's how weddings used to be set up a long time ago, but even then it was rather a waste of space and awkward when someone gave a speech.

As a seminar leader I would never use this style—and yes, this is my opinion. Several of my clients used it until they started working with me. Especially teachers and workshop leaders tried to convince me otherwise.

Their reasoning was strong, but after trying out the recommended style they, too, came to the realization that the U-shape style did not do the job they wanted it to do, after all. They were hoping to create intimacy and wanted to give participants tables to work on. The result? Spilled coffee, unneeded stuff laying on the table distracting everyone and not being able to see the person next to them. Even worse, at the end of the table, communication among participants becomes much more difficult.

In addition, the tables create a physical separation between the seminar leader and his participants and therefore also an emotional separation.

For a trainer it is a nightmare, because you just don't have control of the room at all times. Participants get distracted too easily by their co-participants and have too many opportunities to look away from you. Depending on where you're standing, some will have a good connection with you, while others will not.

I could go on about why not, but that is a waste of paper and pen. Just don't do it—you will regret it, I promise—if not early in the seminar, then at the part where you are promoting the sale of your next seminar or your product.

Boardroom: A trainer's second nightmare. You have little to no control of the participants. Either they have to turn their chairs around to face you, or they have a huge table and a row of participants between them and you; there is just no way you can truly connect with them, not to mention teach them anything. As a trainer, you are an outsider.

You won't have any control, unless you sit with them at the table (and then I hope you are the CEO of that company). Even then, some will see you sideways, some not at all; some will play with their pens, or spill coffee and look at their watches, eager for the boardroom meeting to be over so they can get back to work.

Board meetings yes, trainings or workshops no.

Classroom: I might use this style if I absolutely can't move the tables out of the room and if I have fewer than ten people in the room (so it looks "bigger").

The classroom style does have the advantage of allowing participants to have a computer or paper to write on, but the way my seminars are conducted, I don't want participants to fuss with their stuff, spill coffee or tap their pens on the table. All of these are distractions you can do without. That style also does not give enough flexibility with stage changes. (You will learn what those are, why we have them and how to use them later in the book.)

Once again, the tables are a big barrier between you and the participants. Your chances of great intimacy are not as good as when there is nothing between you and them. We always want to have the opportunity to create intimacy, trust and connection with our participants. All the things you need to create to have an unforgettable seminar.

This style is simply not what high-powered trainers use, so again, don't do it!

Theatre: This is the recommended way of setting up the room; it's the best way for a seminar leader to control the energy in the room. There are only chairs, no tables. It's a much friendlier way of accelerating learning, playing games and clearing the room.

It truly is great for workshops and a great way to engage participants. It is a flexible style: you can use it easily while you have stage changes or call people up on your stage to participate (your audience will love that—especially troublemakers, which I will explain later), or while you have participants partner-share or play games.

There is no tapping on tables and no spilled coffee (in fact you don't want coffee or drinks in your seminar room anyway—water is okay); no one can hide from you or sneak out; there is easy microphone access, easy team access for dealing with hand-outs; and mostly you can see what is going on with your participants at all times. You have control over the room, my friend, and that is exactly what you want!

When using the theatre-style, set up chairs in even numbers, 4, 6, 8, etc. (for partner-shares). No middle aisle, ever: It divides the room into two and drives a wedge between the participants on either side—not a good thing.

If the room is very wide, set up chairs in the middle as a block, and create a double-aisle (with both side aisles slanted towards you). If the room is very long, you can create a break after about ten rows if needed. I like to have my chairs close to each other, but make sure if you have banquet chairs that you do have about two inches between them (they are usually more narrow than regular chairs); otherwise have the chairs touch each other.

Measure 4.5 to 5 feet between the back legs of each chair and the back legs of the closest chair in the next row. I recommend you use a measuring tape (don't eyeball it) and mark where the corners of the chairs go with masking tape (on the floor), so your room, is set up to imply excellence and professionalism! It makes a huge difference. Plus, if the chairs get messed up, which they will, they are easy to put back at the breaks—this tape trick will save you a lot of time.

The side aisle should be wide enough for three people to stand next to each other comfortably—if the room allows it. This way, people can easily access their rows and evacuate the room in an emergency. Also, the microphone-runners can easily pass each other.

Your first row of chairs should be about six feet away from the stage, depending on the room size and stage height. My recommendation is that you go on stage and make sure the distance of the first row is comfortable for you—it can't be too close or too far—it must feel right.

Make sure the rows are straight to imply excellence! I can't say it enough.

Never, ever, set up more chairs than participants. In fact, if you expect 100 people who are unconfirmed, then only put out about 75 chairs and leave another 25 chairs stacked out of sight.

Adding chairs at the last minute always looks better than having rows with empty chairs. In fact, you want to avoid empty chairs at all costs. If there are fewer people than expected, make sure your team encourages participants to move up towards the stage and remove the empty chairs from the back rows before the seminar starts.

If your participants are confirmed, you can set up as many chairs as you have confirmations. But, if someone is late, remember the rule, better to add-on than to have empty chairs—so take the empty chairs away!

The Sales Table—a Big Must

The table for your cash registers, computers for the sale, brochures etc., and where your team sits or stands, should always be at the back of the room or near the exit doors. This way, when participants leave the room they see all the wonderful things you have for sale.

If you sell seminars from the stage, the sales table should still be at the back of the room. This is where you can send participants to fill out applications or sales sheets for your products and services offered. Have your staff well trained to handle the sales smoothly and quickly. Make sure they are able to answer all questions and make the sale easy for your buyers. Don't make it complicated or difficult for your participants to buy your services. This should be a great experience for all involved.

Here are the basic rules:

- Applications and sales sheets should be prepared properly in advance.

- Make it easy for the buyer (credit card and PayPal are perfect for fast and easy transactions).

- Your team must be well trained and ready to answer all questions regarding dates and locations of seminars, and investment (full payment and partial payment options). Allow the team to make decisions and empower them to give the buyer a great experience when purchasing your products. (We'll talk about your team in another chapter—yes, it is that important.)

Stay Hydrated: Water Stations

Water stations should be located on both sides of the room or also at the back of the room, depending how large your seminar is. Never have it outside the meeting room and never at the front where the stage is.

You want participants to be able to quench their thirst without being disruptive to the seminar while it is going on. I prefer water bottles, but no open containers that can spill while we have stage changes or in the midst of doing work. It can be too disruptive.

I also ask participants not to consume alcohol during my seminars. I don't like their perception altered while working with my team or me.

Seminars can be very emotional and we don't need extra stimulants to be part of that. Coffee and tea—as well as snacks—are okay to be served outside of the seminar room during breaks. Especially in Europe where a 4 PM coffee/tea-break is almost a must.

Keep your Seminar Cool

What I mean by that is not just that you should be cool—that's a given—but actually keep your seminar room cool. The perfect temperature is 20 degrees Celsius, which is 68 degrees Fahrenheit.

Why? Yes, this is a big why!

First you don't want the room to be too warm or your participants will get tired easily and will feel exhausted by late afternoon.

Also, with a lot of bodies in the room the temperature can rise very quickly. When you add stage changes that can get very physical—body temperatures can rise even more.

Cooler temperatures will keep everyone awake and actually more comfortable. I always suggest to my participants that they dress in layers.

Also when you are on stage, it gets hot up there. Yes, you too need to stay comfortable. So make sure that your room has an adequate cooling system.

Keep out the Distractions

It is best to rent rooms without windows. In fact, in the U.S. military, there are no windows in their classrooms.

Why?

Because it has been demonstrated that students pay more attention, learn faster and remember more of what they learned when there are no windows.

If there are windows in the room, draw the curtains. Do not under any circumstances open the windows to encourage your participants to look outside. Remember, you are supposed to manage the energy in the room. You will lose that if people start looking outside admiring the beautiful landscape or watching people walk by outside the room.

So, keep those curtains drawn!

Also, keep the doors closed during your seminar and only open them when you want participants to leave the room. With this little trick you will sell more at the end of the seminar.

Toolbox 2—You are only as Good as Your Team

ISN'T THAT THE truth! Never underestimate the value of your team members. They can make or break your seminar. Not only are your team members usually loyal fans and your biggest cheerleaders, you will see that no one can do it on their own. You need help before the seminar and especially—during the seminar.

> *Great things in business are never done by one person. They're done by a team of people.*
> —Steve Jobs

Here are some tips on why you would want to invest the time and effort to train your team members well.

The Value of Having Four Team Members

You must figure out what your magic number of team members is—and why using the right number of team members will make your life so much easier being an awesome seminar leader!

For me, that number is four.

- One team member is your Personal Assistant: He or

she will make your life much easier...I promise. Make sure this person is your right hand and knows what to do, and also understands your vision and why you do certain things. On the day of the seminar you won't remember a thing about taking care of yourself. At this point, you get to focus on delivering the seminar in excellence. And, as a trainer that knows what he/she is doing, you get to create awesome energy in the room for your participants.

Your assistant will make sure you don't forget yourself in that equation. He will remind you to eat and rest, assist you with stuff you might have forgotten and keep the participants from overcrowding you in the breaks. Trust me; you will need the small breaks in between. Your personal assistant will know where your stuff is and will be able to handle last minute emergencies. He will keep you hydrated and keep negative news away from you until you can deal with it. A personal assistant will be your guardian angel throughout the seminar. The truth is you can't and you won't have to do it all by yourself.

- A second team member is your Salesperson: She is responsible for all sales and money transactions. Again, you cannot do everything on your own. Train a responsible team member that does well with numbers and give her the power to make decisions to make your customers happy and manage the payments. Of course, you too can be a big part of the sales transactions; you can help answer questions and create further trust with your customers, but it is much easier if you have some trusted person handle all of that. It also looks more professional if you don't do it all yourself. With time, all your volunteers should be trained to become an awesome sales team for you.

- Another team member should be your Volunteer Coordinator. This person will be responsible for your volunteers. You want to train one person in everything she must know so that your seminar can run smoothly. From dealing with handouts to how the chairs should be set up, how to manage the microphone runners, and how to assist your participants with small issues. Train that person well. (Best: let them read this book.)

Your Volunteer Coordinator will also train your other volunteers. You want to have enough volunteers to handle everything that needs to be handled (that is in the next chapter) but not so many that they fall over each other.

She must treat all volunteers with respect. They are there to be of service, but they are not anybody's personal slaves. This is a huge distinction. I have seen volunteers treated like crap—not a good image for you and your seminar. Plus, unhappy volunteers bring bad energy in the room. So make sure they are acknowledged and cared for.

- Finally, you need a Tech/Music/Energy Manager: You must have a sound system, regardless of whether you have 50 people or 5,000 people in your room.

And it must work well.

Make sure that your tech person knows how to deal with the microphones (and, if at all possible, a headset for you). The person must know what music to play when, especially during the work sessions, breaks, stage changes, etc. Keeping up the energy in the room is a vital part of making your seminar successful. The technical part of your seminar must work—otherwise it is too disruptive.

If you can, have your Tech Manager video your seminars so that you can watch them after the event. It will help you improve the quality of your seminars in record time. You can see all the stuff you do right and all the stuff that needs to improve or change. It is not easy to watch yourself on video (speaking from experience), but you also may be surprised. Regardless of how you feel about it—do it anyway.

How to Train your Crewmembers and Volunteers

The difference between a crewmember and a volunteer is that the crewmember is getting paid, either hourly or on a fixed salary, whereas the volunteer is unpaid. The crewmember is an extension of you. She is a part of your core team and will probably travel with you to all your seminars.

Volunteers don't get paid but do get many perks. They are not obligated to be at your events, but do this to enrich their own lives, better their businesses, learn from you, and be of service to others.

One quality to look for in your crewmembers and volunteers is being a self starter. Still, both need to be trained so the seminar goes well and is successful.

- Train them in advance, not on the day of the seminar. Best—do it the evening before, or even have a general training session that everyone should attend once a year.

- Your volunteers must understand that they have to leave their personal problems at the door. They also must understand that the seminar is for the participants and not for them. Not that they won't pick up great information or hear things they haven't heard before in your seminar, but their mindset must be that they are there to serve others and that is their reward.

- How to find your volunteers? I would only use volunteers that have previously taken the seminar that they are volunteering for. They loved it! They want more and also want to be of service to others. They're getting the chance to pay it forward! You might want to send an email to your database of previous seminar participants and ask if people would like to help you at your next event. You might be surprised how eager people can be. Word goes out fast through Facebook—and who does not want to be part of a winning team? In case this is your first seminar and you don't have graduates that can take the place of volunteers, you can get started by asking friends and family to support you in your endeavor. But don't do it alone.

- Why should they want to be there? Your volunteers will want to have the chance to work with you and your team. At the seminar they will get the opportunity to be of service (karma). They will learn a hell of a lot—I promise. I have hundreds of volunteer hours under my belt. It is not only satisfying and rewarding, I learned, learned, and learned a ton. Nothing is more satisfying and rewarding than being surrounded by like-minded people. I acquired my best friends over the years through volunteer work. Your volunteers will become more successful in their own businesses, because they worked with you and your team.

- All volunteers must be there for the entire seminar. I don't allow volunteers to be seminar hoppers. It is too much work on your part to keep track of who is responsible for what. It is not fair to other volunteers that make the full commitment of their time and energy. And it can be very disruptive to the flow of the workshop and to the participants.

- Volunteers get trained in every task over time, from setting up chairs, to working on the sales table, to coaching participants. I see this as an intern opportunity. This was my path to really learn how to create my own seminars and now how to teach others how to hold great seminars that work well.

- The volunteers need to understand that a simple "yes" will do. I am not there during the seminar to explain to them why they should do things one way and not another way. That is all explained in the training sessions. At the time of the seminar, they must know how to follow directions, do them quickly, and ask questions later.

- Being of service is keeping your eyes and ears open for participants' needs, but not to hinder them in their learning process, i.e. don't fix them: allow participants to process their emotions themselves. This is where seminar leaders need to give explicit training to their volunteers.

- As a volunteer, you get to spend time with your friends, but under no circumstances do you create a coffee meeting at the back of the room while the seminar leader is trying to teach something. A good volunteer is receptive to the seminar leader and pays attention to his/her needs. We will discuss the duties in a minute.

- If you want to pay your volunteers you can give them "seminar dollars" instead of paying them in cash. I like to give them the opportunity to participate in future seminars, so they can eventually take them for free. You can make other arrangements, based on whatever you think they will value.

- I also provide lunch/dinner and regular breaks for my volunteers—but that is up to you.

As we grow older, you will discover that you have two hands, one for helping yourself, the other for helping others.
—Audrey Hepburn

How to Prepare your Volunteers for the Big Day?

There is nothing more frustrating and disempowering for a volunteer than being thrown into the mix of people and not knowing what to do. Volunteers are in general giving, caring and supportive human beings that want to help you and the participants to get the most out of the seminar.

To do so, they must have exact guidelines, information and understanding on what to do and what not to do. Set your volunteers up for their own success. Make sure they too get something out of the seminar, and feel part of a team.

Here are some things that you can do to help them prepare. Meet your volunteers the day before, if at all possible, to communicate to them the basic guidelines and duties. If that is not possible, then at least meet a couple of hours before the seminar starts.

In the morning, have a clearing—i.e. let your volunteers have a chance to leave all their worries and problems at the door. After the seminar, they can pick them up again and take them back home. But keep them out of the seminar!

Help them become inspired and excited about the day.

Work with them to create a "possibility" word or phrase like: love, being of service, compassion, etc. Creating a possibility word means, who can they be for that day for themselves, for the team and for the participants? Allow them to step into their perfect selves.

Help your volunteers understand that they are there to pay it forward—to be of service—and that by doing so they will get big value for themselves in return.

Have the Volunteer Coordinator check in with the other volunteers throughout the day and see how they are doing.

Well-trained volunteers will not be as frustrated and helpless as untrained volunteers.

If little things go wrong during the day (and they will)—the Volunteer Coordinator must discreetly check in with the volunteers and see how they are doing or handling the issues—and do it fast.

In the evening—after the participants have left the seminar room—the Volunteer Coordinator (or yourself) must have another clearing with your volunteers—so they can leave behind the problems that occurred during the day. Discuss how they can avoid these problems in the future. Empower your team: don't tell them, but allow them to solve it on their own if all possible.

Have the clearing be short—if the seminar goes late into the evening, everyone will be tired. But do make sure you let them know the difference they made for you and for the participants. Then let them go home (or to the hotel room) as soon as possible.

What Else Does my Team Need to Know?

Not every volunteer will know everything immediately, especially if they are helping you out for the very first time. So give them little by little good training and responsibility.

Allow them to grow with you and your seminars over time, and also let them know in the process how very much you appreciate them.

Guidelines and rules are important, because ultimately you are responsible for the outcome of the seminar.

If your actions inspire others to dream more, learn more, do more, and become more, you are a leader.
—John Quincy Adams

How to effectively Organize and Distribute Handouts

- Handouts must be distributed quickly and quietly. Prepare them in an outstanding manner. Handouts should be organized by the number of people in a row times how many rows you have. Hand them to the outside person of each row for them to pass them along to the other side of the row.

- Make sure you made enough copies for everyone.

- Your team must know what to hand out and when.

- They should be ready with the handouts at the drop of a hat.

- You might want to have extra writing paper and pens available for your participants to take notes. (That can be part of the registration package.)

Invisibly run the Microphone

- You should have enough microphones to handle the entire room.

- That means a minimum of two.

- Volunteers should walk swiftly up to the person— hand them the microphone turned on—and then kneel besides them (so they don't block the view of the participants) or in the aisles for an easy reach back of the microphone.

How to Handle the Breaks

- Lunch and dinner breaks are there to reorganize the chairs and the room.

- Participants should take their stuff with them when they leave the room for lunch and dinner breaks.

- Bathroom breaks are just that.

- The room should stay closed until about ten minutes before the seminar starts back up.

- Your volunteers should make sure that no trash is left on the floors.

- The sales tables should be neat and organized.

- The water table should be cleaned up (e.g., remove empty glasses), and the water should be refilled as necessary.

- The volunteers should assist participants with any questions they might have to give the trainer a break.

- The volunteers should also coordinate their own lunch/dinner by staggering their breaks—so that not all volunteers are gone from the room at the same time.

- Communicate with another volunteer if you take a bathroom break.

- Volunteers must communicate with the Volunteer Coordinator if they have an emergency of any kind or have to leave the seminar for a period of time or altogether.

How to Support the Trainer in the Room

- Make sure the trainer has everything s/he needs on the stage.

- Volunteers should be ready to do what the trainer asks them to handle.

- Most important: volunteers must pay attention to signals given by the trainer.

- They also should pay attention at all times to what is said.

- Be prepared for handouts and microphone runs.

- Don't start a conversation with a fellow volunteer at the back room—it is distracting to the seminar leader and the participants.

- Conversations should be in a whisper voice or held outside of the seminar room.

How to Support the Trainer and Participants in the Room

- Pay attention to the trainer for handouts and microphone runs.

- Allow participant to do their work in the seminar— don't rescue them.

- Don't try to coach participants unless the seminar leader asks for that task.

- Discourage participants from leaving the room during the seminar—unless it is an absolute emergency.

- Help participants to quickly solve their own issues if needed.

- Smile at the participants—give them courage.

- Be enthusiastic if needed.

- Be supportive with your thoughts and actions.

How to Dress

Simplicity is the keynote of all true elegance.
—Coco Chanel

- I like to have all of my volunteers match—black pants with logo t-shirt or collared shirt.

- Make sure they are comfortable—also that they can move chairs and boxes, etc. if necessary.

- In my seminars—no jeans! But that is up to the seminar leader! If it is a cowboy convention? That's the exception for me—never say never.

- Leave the sexy stuff at home where it belongs.

- Leave your shoes on. I understand after a long day your feet hurt—bring a second pair if needed.

- It's a good idea to bring a second top, just in case an accident happens.

- Have fun!

- Be professional, but enjoy what you are doing.

What do you do When you are all by Yourself?

When everything seems to be going against you, remember that the airplane takes off against the wind, not with it.
—Henry Ford

I would not recommend that anyone do a workshop or a seminar on their own. Ask a friend or a family member to help you until you can afford an employee or find volunteers to help you. Can you do it on your own?

Yes, you can.

But it is a huge challenge—and you can only do it up to a certain number of participants.

SO YOU, YES, YOU…GET YOURSELF SOME HELP!

My last bit of advice is—if you are really alone—follow the rules to the best of your ability, and then make as many exceptions as you need to make in order to successfully lead that seminar. Try to keep it simple and do your personal best.

Most of all, don't let it deter you from giving a seminar—do it anyway!

Toolbox 3—The Basics

You must know about leading a seminar or workshop in a way that will make it memorable and profitable.
—Margit Macchia

Learning versus Teaching

YOU NEVER WANT to come to a seminar with the attitude that "I am going to teach the participants this or that." Instead, come with the attitude that "I am going to present this or that in such a way that they want to learn it."

To do that effectively, you need to know some of the science behind how people actually learn, and you have to understand that people have the capacity to learn in at least seven different ways.

I always compare it to: What would happen if you told a fish to climb a tree? Or if you asked an elephant to fly? Or a humming bird to swim? You wouldn't really get great results, would you? You would conclude that the fish, the elephant, and the bird are all stupid. All this, just because you didn't do your job in asking them to complete the tasks in the way they are each best suited to doing them.

Therefore, I would like you to first understand how people

learn in different ways and what these learning styles are. Then, and only then, do you get to figure out how to incorporate them into your seminars.

This way, you make sure that your material gets digested by every learning type, and your seminars will be successful no matter who sits in your audience.

Let's get started with some basics, understanding the different learning styles.

- Visual learners need so see things like photos, images, drawings, writing, and presentations.

For this type of participant, write on flip charts, use props, and make sure they use their visual senses. Seeing things written down helps them digest information.

- Audio learners need to hear things like music, sounds, and words.

You can effectively use music at the beginning and during breaks for these types of participants. Also repeat what you wrote on the flip chart. You can have participants read out loud what they have written in their writing exercises or have them read it to their partners. You can also have them use their auditory senses in group work, for example.

- Verbal learners prefer words, spoken or written down; they also like to talk.

This is where you give participants a chance to do written work, partner shares, and group shares, and to repeat what you just wrote on the flip chart. In addition, these participants need to hear their own voices.

- Kinesthetic learners must be able to touch things and have physical experiences.

Yup, have them do jumping jacks and give high fives, Anchoring their newfound knowledge with movements can help people remember more of what they learned. Hands-on exercises are important. It has been demonstrated that people learn more easily and faster, and they retain more information when they get to do something, not just hear it.

- Logical learners often include mathematical people, engineers, or IT people.

The material must be presented to them logically, systematically and with reason. Also these learners need to have fun in a seminar, as long as the material is presented for their type of learning style. You must give them time between lectures to think about what was just presented to them.

- Social learners prefer working in groups.

Make it easy for them to learn with other people's interaction. Their motto: "If I can do it with other people, then why should I be doing it alone." So give a lot of opportunities for group interactions and for working together, even if it is just one on one.

- Solitary learners like to read and learn on their own.

That is a reason why in the seminar you make sure that you give solitaires time to work on their own, especially if you are also asking them to participate in group shares. Give lots of bathroom breaks, etc.

A great seminar integrates at least four to five of these learning styles. This way you can be sure that every learning type will get as much out of your seminars as possible. Sometimes it is not possible to do all seven. But when you combine a few, your participants will retain much more of what you just presented. That is why it is so important that you not just talk, but that you design your seminar in an interactive fashion to accommodate all of your participants in a fun and relaxed way.

Accelerated Learning is the Key

Based on the latest brain research, accelerated learning is the most advanced teaching and effective learning method in use today.

What makes it so effective?

It is based on the way we all naturally learn. It does this by involving the whole person, using physical activity, creativity, music, imagery or color to get participants deeply involved in their own learning.

This is what your participants need for optimal learning:

- A positive learning environment that is both relaxed and stimulating, and that provides a safe environment.

- The opportunity to take full responsibility for their own learning.

- The opportunity to collaborate with other learners.

- Variety that appeals to all learning styles.

- Context, not just facts and skills in isolation— because they are hard to absorb and easy to forget.

- Opportunities for doing and for "real-world" immersion, reflection, feedback and evaluation.

Edutainment—to be or not to be Entertaining?

Education and entertainment in combination is the key. We know what education is, right? We know what entertainment is, right? Now imagine putting them both together—that's how we get edutainment!

With edutainment we not only learn something, we learn it in a fun and exciting way! People get to hear what we have to say, and they get to experience the knowledge through dialog, conversation, or exchange with other participants. That is the best way for people to learn and to retain information. As a result, they learn much faster, more easily and more effectively. When we observe children, we can see that they learn with games, playing and being entertained at the same time. Why should adults learn any differently?

By the way, there is a company called Zappos in Las Vegas, Nevada, USA. Their entire culture is based on 80% working time and 20% playtime. Playtime is scheduled so that employees get the opportunity to connect with each other, learn from each other, have fun, explore new and different company jobs, and learn new ways of doing things. That company is growing and thriving. Their employees are loyal and producing record results.

What the Heck is Exformation?

Exformation is a word that the German Learning Scientist, Vera Birkenbihl, created. Vera was one of the leading researchers on the human brain and how people learn best and retain information in the most effective way.

You won't find the word exformation in the dictionary, but let me explain:

In an excellent seminar it is not only about the information you offer—not at all! Of course, the information, i.e. what you are talking about, creates some of the value of the seminar, and it is important. But, you must prepare a great product that your ideal participants want to receive. However, that is not the only thing—accelerated learning is a big part of it.

Exformation must be part of your seminar. What is exformation? It is humanity, rituals, fun, creating excitement, games, plays...everything that makes a seminar unforgettable—everything you are learning here in this book! Exformation goes deep down into the depth of a human being's consciousness.

So use it!

The most Important Rules about Language

- Make sure that you use only language familiar to your participants. If they don't have a clue what you are talking about, how can they follow you, connect with you, or learn from you?

- If you have to use a word that your participants might not know, take the time to explain it and let them know why this particular word is so important in that context.

- Don't take your word knowledge for granted—some participants might not have your level of education.

- Don't use cuss words. This is not a comedy club where you can get away with it. Sometimes when I hear seminar leaders cuss it makes me sad, because it does offend certain people. Guess what, you just lost your sale. It never offended anybody when someone didn't use cuss words.

There are exceptions like Anthony Robbins—and who am I to say he shouldn't use that kind of language? He is the best of the best of seminar leaders. But what I noticed is that he uses it to create an effect or transformation. Still—every time he uses a four-letter word I cringe. You guessed it. I am not a fan of cussing. I know someone can and will say "that is your problem, Margit" and they are right! I do not deny it, but I won't purchase seminars from guys where I know that they are constantly on "the cuss parade." I personally don't like it and I won't buy from them. I simply refuse to spend my hard earned money to hear someone cuss the entire weekend. I say it is my preference, and this is my book I am writing, so I am giving you my advice. Anthony Robbins can get away with cussing—you and I, however, I am not so sure about.

I also know that times are changing, but I am old fashioned. What language you use in your seminars is up to you, but I want to caution you in every way to think carefully about your choices.

Resistance is a Good Thing—or is It?

I would have never believed it, but resistance is a good thing if you know how to handle it the right way! In some way, shape or form, there is a possibility that you will experience resistance from one of your participants. And why not? After all, you might have just shaken up their entire belief system that they are holding on to for dear life.

It might be as simple as a survival mechanism or a feeling or belief that has been with them for many years. How are you going to deal with them? And deal you must.

The best way is to take this opportunity to ask them questions, give them space for their resistance, and most of all, to be compassionate.

Remember, what you resist persists. Listen to them with an

open heart and watch them transform right in front of your eyes. If you give them time and attention, and you explore that resistance with them, then you might turn this person into your number one fan! This is a great opportunity to use your coaching skills and your expertise.

Authenticity—the Truth lies in your Being

You can fool all the people some of the time and some of the people all the time, but you cannot fool all the people all the time.
—Abraham Lincoln

Being authentic with your being, your actions and your words is one of the most effective ways to build trust with your participants. Your authenticity needs to shine through in everything related to your seminar. Otherwise your words will be empty, your participants won't trust you, and you won't be successful over the long run. People might not feel or understand why they don't trust you, but they won't if you are not authentic.

When you create your seminar, speak from your heart. You have done the research. You yourself have probably spent a lot of time in seminars, heard great speakers, and been inspired to create your own program.

There was a time where I was so worried that I might be stealing material from other seminar leaders. Then I read the book *Steal like an Artist* by Austin Kleon. After reading it I actually felt like I had permission to "officially steal."

I felt so relieved.

Let me explain: On the one hand, I knew there is nothing original or new under the sun. It even says so in the Bible (and that was written 2,000 years ago). Especially in the speaking world, there really is nothing new. I was always terrified of copying other people, using other people's material. I just didn't want to repeat something I had heard from someone else, until I realized that I am not repeating other people's material. Instead, I have been gathering information, learning a ton and paying for the information with my good, hard earned money. Now all the information I stuffed into my head, sorted out, put in order, re-thought once more, re-wrote several times, tried out myself, and at last stamped with my own "Margit", voila, became "Margit's Original." By the way, the people that I did learn the stuff from, they too learned it from someone, and that someone learned it from someone else—and so on.

T. Harv Eker said once: "You can freely share my knowledge with anyone, as long as proper credit is attributed to my original work."

Make sure you always give credit where credit is due.

With some of the material I've heard, I actually don't remember anymore where I heard it the first time. The world keeps repeating the same old stuff over and over again, in so many different ways.

My best advice is that the materials you learned, heard, saw—try them out yourself and find out what doesn't work for you and what does. I had to try out for myself what wasn't authentic for me and what was.

I would invite you, too, to do the same.

It's Okay to be Emotional

The best and most beautiful things in the world cannot be seen or even touched —they must be felt with the heart.
—Helen Keller

Sometimes we all get emotional. Don't try to hide it. Allow the authenticity of your feelings come through. Here's that word authenticity again.

I remember in one of my seminars I had a moment of weakness (best thing that can happen to you). I later shared this with my participants and I couldn't help myself—I got very emotional.

It was one of the most inspirational and moving moments I have ever experienced with my participants. I was totally vulnerable and never felt so close to them. It was an experience I have not forgotten. You want to have those special moments with your participants.

It brings the seminar to an entirely new level of intimacy.

Allow Silence in the Room

The most precious things in a speech are the pauses.
—Ralph Waldo Emerson

Allowing silence in the room can feel very awkward, but it is an effective way of communicating. Certain things just can't be said, but through silence they can be communicated. Don't try to fill every silence with your comments. None of us have all the answers, and sometimes it is a great opportunity to give participants a chance to answer their own questions in an effective way.

Silence also gives them time to think, to feel, to experience the information they just received. Give them the gift of silence and let them work it out in their minds. In a workshop not long ago, we had the opportunity to practice fifteen seconds of silence. It was a great exercise because even though it was a little different, we all realized it was no big deal, after all.

It's all about the Energy

Passion is energy. Feel the power that comes from focusing on what excites you.
—Oprah Winfrey

I kept hearing from my teachers that if you want to lead an outstanding seminar, you must learn to control the energy in the room. What did they mean by controlling the energy in the room?

It means you must notice when people get emotionally drained, exhausted, tired, or sleepy, etc. Then you must take action. Action to wake them up, to create positive energy flowing back in the room, or to take them out of their heads which are telling them "right now I am exhausted, sleepy, or tired."

Most of these times happen right after lunch, towards the evening, or when people get confronted with stuff they don't want to be responsible for. Create movement in your room, do stage changes, make some noise, allow people to get up, sit down, twirl, whatever...just ramp up the energy—do what you need to do for the energy to rise again.

Music, dance, exercise and laughter are great energy boosters. The higher the energy, the better the seminar experience.

It's Okay to have Fun

People rarely succeed unless they have fun in what they are doing.
—Dale Carnegie

It is absolutely okay to have fun with your participants. Many seminar leaders think that one should stay on task and that the seminar is strictly about educating participants. After all, they might have paid quite a lot of money for the seminar, and one should take this very, very seriously. I agree, the value, in this case the information (the learning), of the course has to be there. However, you are allowed—even encouraged—to have a great deal of fun.

In fact, the more participants enjoy themselves, the more they will learn and the more they will value it. So have some fun while you are at it.

Harness the Power of Playing Games

By playing games you can artificially speed up your learning curve to develop the right kind of thought processes.
—Nate Silver

Did you know that there is an official pre-school for adults in New York where business managers and CEOs spend the day playing games, singing songs, taking naps and having snacks while figuring out how to run their companies efficiently?

I didn't believe it myself either, until I read it with my own eyes in a newspaper and even heard about it on television. The funny thing about it was that the adult pre-school is very profitable and booked for months in advance. I guess there must be something to it!

Remember Zappos from Las Vegas, Nevada from an earlier section? Zappos has playrooms on every level of the company, a gym that was once the old jail in Las Vegas, and on each elevator a television screen with video games. They allow their employees 20% of their working time to play, learn, socialize etc., and 80% to produce results.

As I mentioned in the last chapter—that company is doing well, very well! They must be doing something right!

What I have seen over and over again is when people are playing games and having fun they produce better results, and are more involved and more focused on what they are doing—even though it doesn't look like it.

Clinton Swaine, the founder of Frontier Training, understands the power of playing games and took having fun with his clients to a new level. He dresses his seminar participants up in costumes and likes to use a lot of props. He became an international sensation with his methods while having a blast regardless of where he is teaching.

So I would like to recommend that you include games and fun

times in your seminars.

Allow grownups to be kids again—at least once in a while. We all appreciate it!

Tell them a Story

You can speak well if your tongue can deliver the message of your heart.
—John Ford

Telling stories is an important part of the communication in people's lives. Growing up, I loved hearing my grandmother's stories. I couldn't get enough of them. Most people can relate to other people's stories; they also get inspired, informed and entertained.

Many times stories can take participants on an emotional roller coaster, happy and sad. Plus, they can tremendously increase your sales at the end of the seminar. That is why many seminar leaders have adopted them and made them part of their programs.

At a gut level, we understand that stories bring us closer to our participants. When we tell stories, we get the opportunity to open our hearts and let others in, and we connect with them on a deeper level.

Haven't you also had the experience that you'd rather listen to a great story than hear boring facts? Don't you agree that we can associate ourselves better with other people's stories than when we hear numbers and words coming out of their mouths? Personal stories are endearing and heartfelt.

I remember at one seminar in Austria, I had a participant on stage that I was assisting in having a breakthrough. For quite some time I wasn't getting anywhere with her, but I was committed to not letting her off the stage until she got it. I became very vulnerable and opened up my heart to her and to the other participants with a very personal story.

The seminar took on a much deeper level of intimacy. She as

well as the others could find themselves in my story. Empathy and caring were brought into the space, and in the end she experienced her breakthrough and her a-ha moment through my story.

Give it a try and build personal stories into your seminars.

Treasure them and allow them to affect your participants in a positive way.

How to Deal with Difficult People

Your most unhappy customers are your greatest source of learn-
ing.
—Bill Gates

I already covered some of this when discussing that resistance is a good thing, but I'd like to add something: Sometimes difficult people just want attention.

Instead of ignoring them and allowing them to keep interrupting the seminar, you have some choices.

You can gently remove them from the room: find an excuse at the earliest break and then either refund them their money and let them know that this seminar is not the right venue for them, or, allow your coaches or staff members, if you have them, to help you solve the difficult situation (the latter, of course, is awesome).

Alternatively, I personally like to take this opportunity to enrich the seminar by giving the culprits exactly what they want. I give them some attention by calling them up on stage and asking them if it would be okay if they shared with us what is bothering them.

At the same time I also ask for permission to coach them. This way I can help them get over their issues and become active and happy participants in the workshop. Whatever you need to do to solve the difficult situation—do it.

Don't let it go or postpone it till later—deal with it in the here and now.

The sooner the better.

Feel Safe with Rituals

People like to feel safe. They also like to have routines and to know over a period of time, what will happen next. We all are creatures of habit. In my seminars I build in some rituals that people can look forward to in the morning, just before they go to lunch or dinner, and again maybe right after they come back from lunch or dinner (especially when the seminar is more than one day long). I also like to have rituals for entertainment, rewards and simple stage changes.

Here are some of the rituals I have observed from other seminar leaders and have used myself on different occasions:

- Many morning rituals start the session with music and dancing, follow the leader, or simple body movements. Clapping out a song is a great way to gather people's attention and to let them know the seminar is about to start.

- Celebrate any occasion: birthdays, anniversaries, un-birthdays, or anything you can think of. It's fun, people like it, and it gets the energy in the room going.

- Some seminar leaders invite participants to come on stage and draw a card from a deck for inspiration.

- Repeating what was taught the previous day can be a great ritual. Whatever you feel comfortable with, start the seminar day in a certain way every day and people will feel more at home.

- After lunch or dinner most seminar leaders like to invite people back into the room with music and encourage them to do some body movements, high energy music—anything that will prevent having participants take their after meal naps in the seminar room.

- One of my favorite rituals that I learned from Callan Rush is: instead of applauding when someone does something great or shares in the room, she establishes at the very beginning of her seminar that she gives out kissing gestures. Participants can choose which ones they would like! Sweet kiss, butterfly kiss, sound-making kiss, bird kiss, and so on. This is not only a fun way to acknowledge participants, but also a great way to involve everyone in the room. It always brings a smile to my participants' faces.

So make up your own rituals, have fun with them, connect with your participants and allow them to feel right at home in your seminar.

Speak to Us

Make sure you connect with every participant in the room—not just with the first or second row, but every row.

How can you do that?

First of all, don't speak over participants' heads. Make eye-contact with one person, then with the next, and the next and so on. Of course, if you have an audience of thousands of people, that might be a challenge. But for most of us, when we get started we don't have thousands of people, but maybe fifty, or a hundred, maybe a few more or less.

What is important is that you do make eye contact with everyone in the room before the first hour has gone by, if not sooner. I also project to the entire room. I don't want to lose people in the back of the room because I am talking to the front row. If I did, people would start checking out psychologically, emotionally and yes, also physically, by simply getting up and leaving the room—and we all know that is not what we want!

It is imperative that you connect with your participants, so the entire room feels connected with you. The earlier you do that going in, the better the conversations will be. The level of intimacy will be very high and very productive.

One more tip, if a participant asks you a question during your seminar, which will happen, make sure that you are not only speaking to him—or even worse going close to him to answer—don't do it. Instead, you want to speak to the entire room. Make sure when in a conversation with a participant, that you take your body to a place on stage where you can see everyone and everyone can see you.

Here are step-by-step instructions on how to do just that.

Participant asks a question.

You repeat the question—make it loud and clear so everyone in the room can hear it.

At the same time, make sure that if that participant, for example, was sitting near the right side, close to the stage, then go to the very left side of the stage. Make sure that you are not pointing your back to someone, but that you can see everyone in the room.

Let her know that this was a great question (so you encourage others to participate too).

Either ask if someone knows the answer or you can answer that question yourself.

Ask if the question was answered to her satisfaction.

If yes, thank her and you/the other participants will give her a round of applause.

If no, ask for more information so that the question can be answered with success.

Now, let's say someone on the left side asks a question and you want to take it.

Make sure you do the same, but move your body to the right side of the stage and repeat the steps above.

If it takes a long time to answer the question, it is okay to move into the middle of the stage when you answer.

Never, ever just talk to one person and shut out the rest of the room.

Practice, practice, practice—it takes time to get used to this format, but it works.

Leave No One Behind

Make sure that your entire room has the opportunity to participate. Sometimes we have those wallflowers that are willing to sit through a few days of seminars and never say a word. They passively observe what is going on, but don't really participate if at all possible.

Become aware of who those are and make sure they, too, get their personal breakthroughs. Silent water is deep. In fact, one of the things I love about Anthony Robbins is that he works so closely with his team that his team finds out very quickly who those wallflowers are, and then makes sure that they, too, get out of the seminar what they came for.

Make sure that you are totally aware of who is in your room and who needs attention (not the attention seekers but truly the ones that are otherwise overlooked). Make sure that they get support from your team as well as from you. No one should ever be left behind.

Account for every Minute

First of all, I would like to suggest to you that you plan out your seminar not only with good value, but also within a great timetable. Allow enough time for your curriculum, questions, coaching, breaks, and transition time. Those are the little minutes here and there that get lost when people are putting their bags under the chairs, finding their seats, drinking their coffee, getting in the room at the last minute, etc.

It is so very important for you to stay within your timeline. People do not like to go to lunch late, or to end the seminar at something other than the agreed upon time. They still might hang around after the seminar for another hour or so, but the seminar itself has to be completed on time.

Over the years, I've heard something like this from several of my students:

> I did really great on time at the beginning of the seminar, and soon I lost track of time, and of course I didn't have enough time to sell my next seminar (or the sales part had to be cut short). I felt the pressure to complete on time, I just didn't have enough time to make a presentation of my products, etc.

Managing your time is one of the most difficult and most important parts of the seminar. But what absolutely must always happen is that you complete the training part on time and leave enough room for your sales presentation. You must be willing to really understand time management and the sales opportunity of a seminar.

Here are some tips for managing your timetable effectively:

- Always start your seminars on time. Don't teach your participants that they can be late and that you will wait for them.

- Keep checking your time schedule throughout the seminar. Make sure you stay on track with it. I have a watch hanging on my music stand.

- Plan for extra transition time in your time budget.

- Before each break, be clear about how long the break is going to be and when you expect participants to be back in their chairs—communicate that clearly.

- If you run short on time because the presentation took too long, then you might have to settle for less exercise or share time.

- When your time is up for a certain section, it is up. Don't allow participants to run your seminar. You need to maintain control of it.

- When you write the seminar, schedule everything. I mean everything: lecture, exercises, shares, people walking on stage, leaving stage, stage changes, lunch, dinner, breaks, etc.

- During a day long, or weekend seminar I also build in some "blank" time just in case I need more time.

Blank time is when I schedule nothing. Once you get the feel for how long you need for stuff, this won't be necessary anymore.

- Never, ever compromise the time for the sale of your next seminar/product.

- Make sure you always end on time.

- If for whatever reason you might really need an extra ten minutes to complete the seminar, ask for permission. Let them know that you didn't manage the time as planned and ask if it is okay to take an extra ten minutes to finish up. Never just keep going and let participants wonder when the seminar will be done.

I know this is a lot of information, but I promise you by the end of the book it will all make sense.

Give Me a Break!

Almost everything will work again if you unplug it for a few minutes...including you.
—Ann Lamott

Give your participants a break on a regular basis to allow them to go to the bathroom, get some fresh air or catch five minutes of shuteye—especially if the seminar is longer than a few hours. My seminars are divided into sections of:

- Learning

- Short bathroom breaks

- One long lunch break (mostly working ones) but still time to relax

- A dinner break

- Mini breaks (like a coffee or tea time)

- Transition to another segment of the seminar

Every 2 to 2.5 hours, allow either a short bathroom break of about ten to fifteen minutes or a lunch/dinner break.

The mini breaks are maybe one to two minutes long with stage changes like standing up, sitting down, shaking out, rubbing shoulders, dancing, etc. They are very important, especially if you see the energy is decreasing in your room. They are no replacement for real breaks, though.

People get very antsy when they can't go to the bathroom or when they get hungry. So plan your breaks well throughout your curriculum—so that your curriculum continues to flow, and the breaks are part of the education.

> *Make sure you have finished speaking before your audience has finished listening.*
> —Dorothy Sarnoff

Develop Your Angel Voice

I do not naturally have a very pleasant voice to listen to, and I am aware of it. I also learned very quickly early on that my voice was suffering. This was before I started investing money, time and effort into my voice.

Even when I spoke only for a short period of time, my untrained voice got very coarse and scratchy. From other seminar leaders I learned quickly that nothing can take the place of a great voice coach. Yes, singing before the event, humming to find my ideal pitch, drinking lots of lemon water and so on—all of these things will help a little.

But, overall, I was clear that if I wanted to use my voice on a daily basis, if I wanted to have a positive impact, and if I wanted to have healthy vocal cords over a long period of time, I had to get a voice coach. I realized soon, that both my career and I would last much longer that way.

So if your voice is adenoidal, breathy, brittle, croaky, dead, flat, grating, gruff, guttural, high-pitched, hoarse, honeyed, monotonous, penetrating, plummy, raucous, rough, small, stentorian, strangled, strident, thick, throaty, tight, toneless, wheezy and/or wobbly—get help.

Your voice will be much more pleasant for your participants to listen to, and you will suffer less from sore throats, etc.

Toolbox 4—The Step by Step Presentation

EVEN THOUGH I would really love to take credit for this part of the knowledge in this book, I can't. Instead, I learned this from participating in many workshops that were simply successful in every way.

The very first time I experienced it was in Los Angeles. Shortly thereafter, many seminar leaders copied the blueprints for this method from each other, and the rest is history. There are many ways to outline your presentation, but if you are just getting started, this is a great way to do so. As I said earlier, I was fortunate enough to work with the best in the seminar business, and I am so grateful that I learned this early in my career. Following this model (I have tried it out many times) it is easy to put together a seminar and to experience success, because it works. Have fun with it!

Before you get started writing your all-day seminar, create a 30 to 90 minute presentation that you can use on your ideal client to try out this formula. Once you have proven to yourself that it works, you can move on to bigger pastures and create a one-day, three-day or weeklong seminar.

The basic formula is always the same. A one-day seminar is just an accumulation of several 90-minute presentations. The same goes for a weeklong seminar. Take a look at it, create your first presentation and the rest will follow.

The success of your presentation will be judged not by the knowledge you send, but by what the listener receives.
—Lilly Walters

What to Do and What to Say?

When you first get on stage, you say nothing and you do nothing. You just look at your participants, and you scan the room from the right to the left and from the left to the right. See who is sitting there. Whom will you spend the next hour, day or weekend with? Whom did you invite to be part of that amazing experience? This will create suspense, and you are off to a great start.

No, this is neither the time nor place for you to introduce your-self—this is the time to further make your participants curious. Demand attention and participation right out of the gate. Here you ask your participants a couple of questions. The best way is to ask pairs of questions that seem to be in opposition to each other. Here's what I mean by that:

- Who in the room lives here in xyz?

- Who decided to come from…?

- Who wants to get really happy?

- Who is okay with staying miserable?

- Who knows how to….?

- Who has no idea?

The main reason you do this is for everyone to get the chance to raise their hands at least once. Immediate involvement of the participants! Curiosity as to why you wouldn't introduce yourself first! This is a very effective way to start your seminar—the technique has been tried and proven by the best of seminar leaders. You don't have to reinvent the wheel!

Then you follow with your name and the name of your workshop.

> *My name is Coach Margit and I would like to welcome you to 'The Trainer's Toolbox Weekend Seminar.'*

It should be an enticing or a tantalizing title. Say it with a lot of excitement. Hey—your participants are in the perfect place to solve their problems.

Why wouldn't you be excited for them?

After that you start to connect with and warm up your participants.

> *I am so glad you are here. I know that there are a million places you could be right now, and you chose to spend the next hour (day, weekend) with me and my crew, and for that I would like to thank you in advance.*

How does that sound? Let the participants know you are happy that they are there with you. That they are giving you their most precious gift—their time.

At this point, if at all possible, thank whoever invited you to speak in front of their people. The HR department, if it is a company, or a specific person. If you got invited to a club or organization, make sure you are grateful for the opportunity, so thank the president, secretary, etc.

By now the participants are going to want to know "What's in it for me?" And now you get to tell them. Don't drag this out. Let' them know: "Today you will learn the following: 1... 2... 3..." You do not have to tell them the entire seminar day, or the entire weekend curriculum. Give them a three point overview to put them at ease, so they know they are in the right room, listening to the right seminar leader that will give them information, knowledge, and training to help them move forward in their lives.

And now a very important question gets thrown into this dialog:

> *Before we get started with the workshop/seminar is it okay if I tell you a little about myself?"*

Make sure you ask your participants if it is okay for you to do that. Ask for permission. You must earn the right to be their seminar leader. (This is so important that I gave this topic "Earn the Right" its own section right after this outline).

They must acknowledge that part. This way, they will pay better attention to what you are about to tell them. And your job will be much easier.

When you are about to finish your story, the second part is the most important—the transition from your story to what's in it for you?

> *Enough about me, this seminar is about you, so let get started, is that okay with you?*

PS: Each time I ask a question I raise one of my hands and wait for an answer by them nodding, or raising their hands or just a simple yes. If for some reason I don't get a response, I will ask the opposite question, "...does anyone not want to get started?"

This usually provokes a humorous response, but I get the point across that I am demanding an answer when I ask a question.

What's in it for Me?

This is the part in your presentation where you let participants know in one or two sentences what they are going to get out of that seminar.

What are the three biggest issues they would like to have solved in their lives to ease their pain? What are the three issues that will help them live better lives? What are the three issues that you will present to them that will make all the difference for them?

Here, you truly must know and understand your ideal client.

Why Should your Participants Listen to You? Earn the Right

When you ask your participants if it is okay for you to share a little about yourself, you get the opportunity at that point to convince them that you can solve their problems or pain, that you are the expert, and that you have gone through a transformation yourself so you can understand their issues.

Data and facts are no good here.

You must take your participants through an emotional story about yourself that explains why you became the expert in what you are talking about. It is also an opportunity for you to start connecting with your participants on an intimate level.

Earning the Right is usually a story about yourself that has three parts:

Part 1: You as the expert: How is your life now—i.e., what success do you have now that your audience wants to learn how to do, live or be?

Part 2: But, it wasn't always that way: Let them know that you too had a time of struggle, a learning curve, and ups and downs, and where you learned these tools to help yourself.

Part 3: And this is why you want to share your experience and knowledge. This is why you are the trainer. This is why you want your audience to have what you learned from your days of struggle. I heard this concept explained for the very first time by Callan Rush (Magnetize Your Audience®). She calls it the Turning Point Story.

Callan and I worked together for the same company. One night I asked her to help me with a speech I had to give the next morning. Working into the night, she shared with me that when I introduce myself I get to take my audience on a roller coaster. I get to connect with them on an emotional level and the same time let them know that I am the expert in helping them out of their pain.

Make this story short, but take the time to enroll your participants into your life, and especially into what's possible for them. "If I can do it—so can you". You just established trust with them by being authentic and open.

Plus, that allows you to have them see you as the expert.

But it's not about me, but YOU—so let's get going! Are you ready to get the seminar off the ground? Everybody, yes? Who isn't? (Again the two opposing questions.)

Isn't that fun?

Craft the Seminar

People get overwhelmed when you tell them too much too soon and all at once. They can only register so much at any one time.

It is therefore of the utmost importance to space out the information logically and add in a lot of other stuff that we already spoke about in previous chapters, i.e. exformation, rituals, stage changes, breaks, etc.

Remember, they only have an attention span of about 7 to 8 minutes before their minds start to wander. That is why it is so important to plan your seminar out with all of the information of this book. You want to keep your participants excited about what they are learning.

The best seminar management is for you to create information sections that are each about 45 to 90 minutes long. If you have an all-day seminar, divide the hours of the seminar by 90 minutes and you will know approximately how many sections you will need.

Don't forget to add breaks, lunch, dinner, teamwork, room shares, etc. into your timetable. It's as easy as that.

Choose One Topic at a Time

Choose a significant topic and then within that topic choose three sub topics.

Let's say you choose: "Losing 10 pounds in 30 days or less." That is your seminar topic. The three sub topics could be: "Why people are overweight? Are you a sugar or a fat burner? How can you, too, have sweets and still lose weight?"

Each topic can be organized in a very easy and simple way— you need to address the what, the why, and the how.

WHAT?

- Explain the topic. What is it? Help your participants understand the topic. In other words create an unveiling of the very thing they want to understand or learn.

- In case it's not obvious, explain what the topic means. Maybe you want to look it up in the dictionary.

- Give your participants a practical example: stories, photos, examples of the problem, history, etc.

- Also let them know what it is not. Explain to them what the topic is not and if possible why.

WHY?

- Explain why it is so important for your participants to understand the topic. What could happen if they don't understand it? Show them what pain they might have to endure if they don't solve this problem. Remember, the bigger the problem, the better the sale afterwards.

- Use real stories and examples to make it very visual for your participants.

- Tell a personal story if at all possible.

- If you have statistics, numbers that are real, educate yourself about them and present them to your participants. They are a powerful tool used as a wakeup call, to back up your stories, to make them real, to convince your participants to make changes, and to give them value in your seminar.

HOW?

- Let your participants know how they can immediately fix their issues, handle their topics, and use this knowledge in real life.

- Give them strategies, plans, notes, etc.

- Give them knowledge they can use right away.

Examples might include, "Three food-groups you should avoid to lose weight faster" or "Five mistakes people make to yo-yo with their weight."

A Side Note that Can Significantly Enhance the Experience of Your Participants

As part of each section you can include writing exercises, room discussions, team discussions, room shares, worksheets, etc. So let's look at a possibility of a segment:

- Give your participants a writing exercise—while you drink tea!

After that…

- Make them have a partner share—while you drink tea!

And then …

- Have a room share—now you get to pay attention!!!

What is a writing exercise, a partner share, or a room share? Why would I want to have them? And how can I manage them?

These things will be explained in the next chapter.

And now I would like to reveal two critically important secrets to you!

You might not want to believe me—but it is true! A very successful seminar leader (a *very* successful one) told me that several years ago—and out of my own experience I need to let you know two things you need to do well if you want to be successful as a workshop or seminar leader.

Here comes the secret:

DRUMROLL, please!!!!

Secret #1: The energy in the room must be managed at all times - keep it high.

Secret #2: The more you sit in your chair and drink tea, the better the seminar will be!

And that is the reason why you must learn this next part by heart: You must know how to give your participants writing exercises, how to have them do partner shares, and then how to use the opportunity to have room shares for people to connect and for you to coach them right there and then. This truly is what gets participants excited about the seminar.

So now let's get back and get started with the exercises.

Writing Exercises—Reflecting on Problems and Successes

I like to use worksheets that are easy to fill out, yet allow participants to reflect.

When giving participants writing exercises, we allow them to reflect on their problems, issues, successes, pain, or anything we want them to work on by themselves. I prefer worksheets that have been very carefully prepared with questions that stimulate participants' mental and emotional state. Sometimes it can be just a simple inventory of facts that pertain to their lives.

Here is a great way to get them started:

- Let them know that they are going to do an exercise on their own.

- "I'm giving you…minutes to complete this exercise. Ready… set… go…"

When the minutes are complete:

- "Did everyone complete…?"

- "No?"

- "Okay, how about I give you another thirty seconds to complete."

Do not give them too much time. It will only cause them to lose focus and or get distracted with chitchat.

After they are done you can either directly lead into the partner share or you can have a couple of people share with the whole room what they have written down and then lead into the partner share. I usually wait with the room share until after the partner share. It all depends on the time I have available.

Partner Shares—Manage your Participants

After your participants have worked on their own exercise, questionnaire or whatever you had them work on, it is a great idea to give them the opportunity to share this with a partner. This enables them either to let the burden go, or to get feedback and for some to see that they are not the only ones with the problem, or to (sometimes) get help from their partner.

This also works in groups of three or four. Sometimes we have several people work on a subject and then they share their outcome.

This is a great way to manage and prompt partner shares:

- "Please find a partner."

- "If you don't have a partner—please raise your hand, look around, and find someone that also has their hand raised."

- "Please sit together."

- "Now let's choose a partner A and a partner B" or "Partner A has long hair, and partner B has the shorter hair," etc.

- "Now share with your partner what you have written down when I tell you."

- "I give you a total of…minutes. Each partner gets…minutes.

- "I will tell you when it's time to change with your partner."

- "A begins" (or B, or the person with the longer, shorter, darker, lighter hair etc.).

- "Let's get started, please begin."

- "Please change partners."

- "Please thank your partner for sharing."

It looks pretty easy, and it is, but it does take practice, so let's begin practicing—and don't forget to drink your tea while all this fun is happening in the room.

Again, we have accomplished another task, and now we want

to bring the entire group of participants together, have them relate to each other, give them the opportunity to learn from each other, and also get the opportunity to be coached by you. Always make sure you ask for permission before you coach anyone in the room—either at the beginning of the seminar as a general permission or before you start coaching an individual. It helps participants to be more open to getting feedback and it supports the coaching process.

Manage your Room Share with Eloquence

I know, I keep saying this part is very important throughout this book, but they all are. The more you follow the guidelines, the better you will be able to connect with your participants, and the participants will be able to connect with each other. You need to give people time to share and yet you need to manage the time. You need to manage the energy in the room. You also need to coach, direct and redirect your participants. For many people this is one of their favorite parts of the seminar. It can be very touching and moving. Many tears have been shared, as well as many insights, joy, laughter, inspiration, and a-ha experiences. You, as the seminar leader, get to make this all happen.

This is a great way to get the process started:

- "Who would like to share what they have written down or what they just learned about themselves?" Put your own hand up, so the participants feel at ease and feel invited to raise their hands.

- "Yes, please, the lady with the red blouse in the second row."

- "Would you please stand up?" This is where the microphone runners come in.

- "Please speak into the microphone. Thank you."

- "Thank you for sharing—for the sake of time is it okay if we hold the applause for the end of all sharing?"

- If you have plenty of time, try out the "kisses applause" or any other form of recognition again. Have fun with it.

- "Who else would like to share with us?"

- "How many of you can relate to that?"

- "Thank you."

- "Now can we have a round of applause for everyone?"

Remember that you need to remain on the stage and work with the participants while the room share is going on. I mentioned it earlier in the book—but just in case you forgot: you don't want to lose the participants and the energy in the room. If a participant to the right of the stage stands up, you must go all the way to the left of the stage, make sure your body is turned in such a way that you can see everyone more or less. If a participant to the left of the stage stands up, you must go all the way to the right of the stage.

If there are questions and you need to speak to everyone in the room, go to the middle of the stage to first repeat the question and then answer it.

Many times group work (more than two people working together) or room work (the entire room is involved) is expected in workshops and seminars. It provides certain people and learning styles a big comfort.

Choose your exercises well and keep in mind why and what outcome you want to have after the participants are done with the exercise. Also keep track of time. Manage your time well, so you won't get into trouble later on.

Get your Audience Involved on Stage

I like to bring participants up on stage for several reasons. First of all and most important, it makes them feel special. Second, it can facilitate a stage change. Last but not least, they are also a great help for writing on the flip chart or doing something you can't do yourself or where you don't want to use an assistant. Plus you always have fun with them.

- Ask for a volunteer. Most of the time you won't have any problems with choosing one of the participants who are eagerly raising their arms.

- Always have them walk up the side steps onto the stage. Never allow them to jump on or off the stage. They can get hurt and so can you.

- Ask them their name and ask the participants: "Let's say hello to…"

- "Thank you for coming up and helping me" or "Thank you for volunteering."

- Let them know what they have to do.

- Give them something if possible (t-shirt, cup, CD) as a reward; a great hug can be fine too.

- "Let's thank...for helping us out."

- Walk them to the edge of the stage and wait until they sit down before you return to the seminar.

You just had a ton of fun with your volunteer and your participants. Fun is always good, especially with a group that might not easily be amused.

Handling Questions and Answers

If you have a question and answer section as part of your seminar then please consider the following.

- Ask participants to hold their applause until the end of the session. Otherwise it takes too much time and is disruptive.

- Ask if anyone has any questions and raise your hand the same time. This gives the participants the hint to raise their hands if they have a question.

- Make sure the person asking the question stands up. Hand them a microphone if one is available, and then make sure they use it correctly.

- Repeat their question.

- See if anyone in the room has the answer (if that is appropriate for the seminar). Then repeat the answer, to make sure everyone can hear it. If no one has an answer? Hopefully you have it!

- Ask the person that asked the question whether that answered their question.

- If yes, they can sit down.

- Then ask if there are other questions or move on with the program.

- If no, coach them to get their answer.

- If you don't know the answer, be honest: don't make something up. Tell them you don't know, but you will find out at the next break, or again, see if someone else in the room might have the answer.

- Set a time limit to the question and answer section.

- Thank the audience for their participation.

- If you know that you are only going to answer one person's question then it is important to thank them directly after it.

Seed Your Seminars

What is seeding? I think of it as a beautiful garden and from it, at some point I want to harvest healthy vegetables or beautiful flowers or whatever my heart desires.

First I must plant a seed. Then, I get to water it, and allow sunshine to help it grow. Mostly I have an expectation that whatever seed I planted, that's what I'll get to harvest later. If I plant a watermelon seed, I get to harvest watermelons and not grapes or potatoes.

In your seminar you get to do the same. You get to plant a seed of your future seminar/workshop/product (that you would like to sell) into the mind of your potential customer. You mention it lightly in the midst of your presentation when it is appropriate. Then throughout the seminar you get to water that seed by explaining the benefit of the product, how the customer could best use it, and why someone would want to have it.

Later on when you get to your sales part of the seminar, you get to harvest the seed because your participants already had the opportunity to allow that seed to grow in their minds—that it might be something beneficial to them. So the product or service is not something totally new, but is familiar to the participant.

That makes the sales part much easier.

Now, how do you close the irresistible offer and help participants choose your product with joy?

That is explained in Toolbox 5.

Toolbox 5—To Sell or Not to Sell, that is the Question

Develop your dreams, advertise your goals, execute your plan, close the sale.
—Michael Dooley

DO YOU FEEL comfortable or are you actually terrified of selling your own products/services?

This chapter, as well as the Encore section of this book, is dedicated to my trusted teacher, T. Harv Eker, the genius behind the world's best sales and marketing seminars.

I not only had the privilege to work for and with him, I had the chance to learn from him while watching him do sales presentations just like the one described here below, creating well over a million dollars of weekend revenue.

There are definitely some sales maniacs out there, but most of us entrepreneurs, small (or large) business owners, coaches, teachers, etc. are not the best at selling our own products/services. After all, you didn't study to be a sales person, you studied to be a coach, therapist, trainer, consultant, real estate agent, doctor, lawyer, communication expert, and so on. But you do offer great products or services, and it is worth your time to learn how to sell them, to make an impact on the world or in your neighborhood—the easy way.

Fortunately, there is a template for being a great salesperson on stage. No, I didn't invent it myself. I, too, learned it and even though I didn't believe it at first, it works over, and over, and over again. Once I understood the template and practiced it, it became second nature. And, to my surprise I noticed that many of the best seminar leaders use the same strategy to sell their products or services.

Here we go—here is "The Most Successful Sales Template" everyone should practice and use to sell their own products and services. I first saw it at a three-day seminar in Los Angeles. Slowly, I saw many other seminar leaders copy this way of selling. Now most of them can't imagine doing it any other way. It is honest and smart, and it works!

Selling is for many people a terrible word, but here is how I see it: if you have a great program or product—first of all, you want your clients (customers, patients, participants) to have that program or product—after all, you want them to benefit from it. In fact, if you don't sell it to them, whom are you hurting most, yourself or your clients? Both!

Your clients won't be able to benefit from your awesome program or product if you don't sell it to them. Think about it, it would almost be stingy of you. Wouldn't you want to buy your own product? Don't you think your product is worth sharing? So why would you want to keep it from the very person (your ideal client!) that could benefit from it?

Second, you've earned the right to make an awesome living. You either worked hard to produce the program or product, or you put in time to research the product, and to find a great source, and now you are taking the risk to purchase it in advance (or not), and taking the time to market it so you can resell it. In other words, you earned the right to sell it.

So, stop being stingy! Handle your fear of selling, i.e. making an offer, and let's get going.

A Step by Step Sales Offer that Works: How to Sell the Easy Way!

The biggest mistake sales presenters make is providing the wrong information—failing to bridge the gap between what the speaker is selling and the benefit to the audience. They provide information the audience does not care about.
—Ethan Rotman

Here is the template, which I will explain further (and let's assume for now that the product is a seminar)...

Prepare the logistics.

Seed throughout the seminar.

What problem are you solving for your client?

What solutions are you offering?

Ask for permission to tell them about your seminar.

Thank participants for allowing you to make them an offer. Name the offer!

For whom is it suited? For whom is it not and why?

Calculate the worth of the seminar for your client and set a value.

What will they get or learn from it?

What are the main reasons they should purchase the seminar?

What is the price of the product?

Share some testimonials or a story.

You are offering a seminar—where and when will it be?

What is the "Special Seminar Price" and the reason for this price?

What is the bonus—something they get if they purchase the program now?

What are the limitations? Create a lack!

What guarantee do you provide?

Invite them to take action now—close the deal!

Allow registration to take place.

Thank the participants for registering or purchasing the seminar.

Follow this sales section with a powerful ending.

Let's take a look at that sales template a little more closely:

Prepare the logistics.

Make sure that your team is ready with order forms and payment possibilities for participants to purchase your next programs.
    Your team should also be able to answer questions about different payment methods and dates/times of your programs.

Seed throughout the seminar.

I know you didn't forget about the seeding throughout the seminar, so what's coming is no news for your participants. Make sure you always only seed for one product or seminar at a time. Let's say you have a seminar over several days. Don't seed for several programs at once, focus on one program, make an offer, sell it and then seed for another program and so on.

What problem are you solving for your client?

This is the part where you make your participants aware of the problems they want to have solved. Remember, you get paid for solving your clients' problems, aka pain.

So yes, you must know what keeps them up at night. And that is the place where you repeat their pain so they can identify with it and start to agree that they don't want to live with their pain anymore.

> How many of you would like to lead seminars, but don't know how to get started?

> How many of you are frustrated with the latest on-line technology?"

> How many of you just can't lose weight and keep it off?

And so on…what is your ideal client's biggest pain?

Have 7 to 10 sentences ready that pertain to one big problem. Also, what was your seminar all about just now? You solved some issue, right? Once these issues are solved, other issues come to the surface. Now you want to solve those issues and when those are solved, yet other issues will come to the surface.

The list of seminars will keep growing until your participants have all their issues, problems, and pain taken care of. Hint: There is always a next problem.

What solutions are you offering?

It doesn't have to go necessarily in the direction of pain. You can show all the pleasure they can receive by participating in your next program. What's in it for them? Why would they want to be in your next seminar? How wonderful will it be to have their problems solved once and for all?

Ask for permission to tell them about your seminar.

First you want to ask if it is okay to introduce your products to them, and then educate them about what you are offering. Share with them why you want them to have the product. This is not about selling something: this is about educating your participants on what is available for them, so their problem can be solved once and for all.

> *Is it okay if I tell you a little bit about my program that would help you to never be frightened again of talking on stage? That would help you let go of being frustrated with the latest online technology? That would help you lose weight and keep it off, once and for all?*

Get it?

Why do we want to ask our participants for permission? Because silently they are already giving us a "yes, yes I am going to listen; yes, I might consider what you have to say." Your participants won't put up a wall before the offer can even be made. Therefore, they will pay better attention to what you say, and they won't see it as a sales pitch, which it is not anyway, but it could be taken as one.

Thank participants for allowing you to make them an offer. Name the offer!

> *Thank you for allowing me to introduce to you "Being on Stage without Fear."*
> *Thank you for allowing me to introduce to you "Mastering On-line Technology."*
>
> *Thank you for allowing me to introduce to you "Losing weight and keeping it off."*

You want to take this opportunity not only to thank them for their generosity of being willing to listen to you, you also get to introduce the name of your product with a tantalizing title.

For whom is the program suited? For whom is it not and why?

We want to let them know which of the participants should not be attending the following program and for whom it would be great. And why!

> *This program is great for people who want to learn to speak on stage with ease. Who want to stop questioning themselves if what they have to say is not valuable. This program is valuable for people that want to go the easy and fast track in the seminar world.*
>
> *Whom is the program not for? It is not for you, if you already know it all; if you are not open to learning; If you have no intentions of introducing your program or product to your potential clients; if you have no intentions of increasing your sales; if you don't want to take the time and look at other possibilities.*

Are you getting the drift?

The part about whom it is not for is as important as the part about whom it is for! It allows you in a different way to inform your ideal client that this program is for him/her, and even more important, sometimes people just don't want to—not be able to do something.

Calculate the worth of the seminar for your client and set a value.

Now we want to calculate the worth of the program and set its value: One great way to do it is to compare your program to other programs out there, that are very high-priced. Alternatively, and I prefer this approach, is to calculate my hourly rate and the time I will be spending with the participants at the seminar.

Let's say my hourly rate is 300 dollars for coaching and at the three-day seminar I calculate about 12 hours a day or more, i.e. 36 hours. Then I would value the seminar at 10,800 dollars. I use that figure and write it on the flip chart as a Seminar Value Price with a black big marker. (Remember when we talked about flip charts and big markers?)

Why do I do that? Because I want participants to not only hear the number, but also to see it, so that it will sink in that this is the value they are getting. In their minds, they are also thinking right now, "I can't afford it"—so when the price goes down in the very next few minutes, it will be a relief for them.

I would charge that if I were teaching just one person. But of course if I have a room full of people my total price of $10,800 just got reduced to a lot less per person, because I have a lot of people paying for that value.

In the end, I can make more money, when enough people sign up for that seminar, but each person will pay less.

What will they get or learn from it?

Now go back and direct your energy and focus on the participants. Share with them what they will get out of the seminar if they participate in it. How can they profit from being in your seminar? "What's in it for me?" That is what they will be asking themselves.

You might think: isn't this the same as number 7? Yes and no. Yes, it will be the same content; no, I will use different kinds of words and sentences. People have to hear the same content more than once to have it sit firmly in their minds. In fact, research has proven that people need to hear or be exposed to the same information up to seven times before it will sink in.

Here you don't focus on the pain anymore, but what they get out of it—take them to the possibility of having their problems solved and their pain removed. Remember you are the bridge between the pain and pleasure. You take them from being scared to being confident on stage. From being broke to being financially free. From being fat to living a healthy, thin lifestyle. And for being the bridge you deserve to be paid, and paid well.

What are the main reasons they should purchase the seminar?

These are the three main reasons you want to be part of this next seminar:

- *You will never be afraid again of being on stage.*

- *You will inspire and motivate your participants.*

- *You will sell and market your product/service with fun and ease.*

What is the price of the product?

At this point you will write the price of the seminar on the flip chart. That is the out the door price you would charge anyone that walks up to you and says: "I want to attend your seminar/workshop."

Cross out the old value price on the flip chart and write your website/brochure price underneath with another colored big marker. In the minds of the participants you just created a big relief. Even though this price might still be a big stretch for some, it could be reachable—and in their minds they are already considering purchasing your seminar/product.

Please be honest about this price. It should be the same all the time—fluctuating with this price is dangerous. The world is a small place and people talk.

Share some testimonials or a story.

If you already have people sitting in your room that have taken your other seminars, or maybe some of your old students are volunteering and helping out. That is a great time for them to speak up and give you some awesome testimonials.

> *Before the seminar my life was like this...then I took the seminar, I learned A.B.C. and now my life is like that.*

> *Before, my skin was like this...then I started to take [name of product] and now after this amount of time I stopped having blemishes and acne.*

You also can include a personal story of your own if you don't have people in the audience that can give you a testimonial. Make it heartfelt so that people can see the value/difference and understand why they should consider purchasing the seminar.

One of the seminar leaders I worked with read from a sheet of paper several testimonials he received over the years. It can be as simple as that.

You are offering a seminar—where and when will it be?

Now is time to let your participants know where and when the seminar will take place.

If you don't have the exact date and place that is okay. Don't sweat it.

I remember sitting in a seminar of Peak Potentials and T. Harv Eker was on stage selling a seminar (it wasn't written as of then, which I found out later). In the break he overheard people talking that they wanted a seminar that offered a certain topic, and he knew that if he offered it—they would buy it. Why not?

He had no time, no place and no details about the seminar. He just said something like it would be in the spring of next year.

People purchased it like hot cakes! They trusted him, they knew that this would be of great value, and it hit a soft spot in their hearts.

The seminar was called "Never Work Again."

What is the "Special Seminar Price" and the reason for this price?

Let your participants know that you are going to give them a special price if they book the seminar today. Also tell them why you can offer them the special price: maybe it's because a lot of them are going to buy the course? Or maybe it is being taught for the first time? Or maybe you have only a few places left?

Now write on the flip chart the special price of your product or seminar. Make sure you use different color markers (write this price with big numbers in RED, circle it!)

And again, you cross off the old prices. This is called the indoor price offer. You want as many participants as possible to make up their minds immediately and take your offer—to enable that to happen, you lower the price one more time. They get this price only if they make a purchase today. Once the seminar is completed the price goes back to the normal outdoor price.

Please stay true to yourself with this rule. People talk and the word would get back to you very fast, if you don't stick to that rule. This is the lowest price at which you are willing to sell your program including the bonus.

What is the bonus—something they get if they purchase the program now?

Now you offer them the icing on the cake. Usually bonuses are not a big deal, unless you want them to be. It is just something extra that will help your participants make up their minds and overcome all their negative communication (in their own minds) about why they shouldn't purchase your product.

- You can give two people admission to the seminar for the price of one—family members (children, spouse).

- Or the second person—usually family members or business partners—get the seminar for 50% off if they take it at the same time.

- Or you can give away books, CDs, webinars, coaching...

- The bonus is something of value to the participants where the deal (including the indoor price and the bonus) is so good, they just can't say no anymore. This is what some seminar leaders call an irresistible offer. The value becomes so big in your clients' eyes, that saying no to this opportunity becomes out of the question. The offer has become too good to pass up.

What are the limitations? Create a lack!

How do we do that? Have you ever gone to a sales event and there was only one blouse on the rack in your size and color? Maybe it was something you'd been looking for and someone else had her hands on it? How did that make you feel at that moment? Didn't you think in secret "I hope she puts it back even just for one second so I can grab it?" Yes—we always want what we think we can't have.

Calculate in advance how many of the seminar/workshop seats or products you would like to sell at that seminar and then let the participants know how many you have available. Please be honest. If you say ten, then it has to be ten. I know for myself, I can't sell 100 coaching sessions in one seminar; I couldn't manage them, so I have to be clear about how many I can offer to be able to be true to myself.

This is not about manipulating people; this is about managing your time and value, and being honest with yourself about what you can handle. And yes, it does help participants make up their minds quicker. You know sometimes we just have to help people make decisions that we know will benefit them greatly. Many of us have big conversations about why we don't deserve things, or why it is okay for others to do that, but not for us. As a coach many times I see people would rather help others than themselves. So if you think about this too, you're really just helping your participants to make up their minds for their own good.

What guarantee do you provide?

Many of today's seminar leaders give a 100% money-back guarantee with their own conditions attached to it.

If you have a five-day seminar and after the first day they don't want to be part of the seminar anymore—they get their money refunded.

You have 48 hours to think about it and get a full refund if you change your mind

Or, you don't want it—no questions asked.

Last year, I participated in an online seminar. The guarantee was that if I completed the 30 days and didn't feel I got any value out of it, I would get a 100% full refund. The condition was that I had to complete all homework, had to be on all calls, and I had to look into the seminar leader's eyes and tell her that it wasn't for me and why. Pretty awesome. Worth giving a 100% refund guarantee any day.

It is totally up to you: Figure out what you are willing to do to make it easy for the buyer to have no purchasing regret, to feel safe and secure handing over their credit cards. It will put your participants at ease.

Invite them to take action now—close the deal!

Now invite people to take action. Give them sign-up sheets and allow them the time to fill them out. Invite them to register today, not tomorrow or next week. If you wait that long—it won't happen. Remember your ideal clients are in front of you right here, right now, and they came because they felt you had something to offer to them. You can provide them the solution to their problem. They really do want your seminars.

Many times their lack of self-worth, or money/time conversation will not allow them to do what is best for them. So if you are scared to invite them to take this opportunity, what happens? Neither their lack of self worth nor your fear will serve you. You must take a stand for your clients; you must help them cross the bridge, take the chance and help them make the decision to take this opportunity now. I am not talking about being a (stereotypical) used car salesman, selling them something they don't want or need (or something that is not of value, broken or just simply a piece of crap).

What I am talking about is that you have something to offer, you know that your participants need this next product to help them move ahead in their lives, and you have offered to them a great deal, so they can have what they need and want! You already gave them their monies worth with the presentation, so please go for it. Invite them to take action now and then allow it to happen.

If someone doesn't register or purchase your product, that is okay too. They just weren't ready then.

Allow the registration to take place.

But let them know that the seminar is not over and that they have X minutes time to get back to their seats, because more exciting stuff is planned.

Never make this sales offer the last thing on the menu. Why? You don't want participants to leave, thinking it is done.

Participants get to stay a little longer for the finish of the seminar, and a powerful finish it will be!

Thank the participants for registering or purchasing the seminar.

When the participants are back in their seats, thank them for registering or purchasing your product. If you know a lot of the people purchased it...

How many of you will be joining me at that next event?

Thank you, we will have an awesome seminar together.

Follow this sales section with a powerful ending.

Get back to an awesome seminar and complete it powerfully with lots of energy and fun. You can have another session or you can end the seminar then. I personally like to give more value, so participants feel that they made a good decision with their purchase - which they did. Blow their minds one more time with the value of your seminars.

If you want, you can let them know before the end of the seminar that the indoor price is good until everyone has gone home. It depends on whether your next seminar is sold out or not. I assume it will be after you have learned this method, because it works!

Important: Now that you have the ground rules of the sale, I would like to give you some advice: Make sure that this sales structure fits your personality.

What do I mean by that? Some people are very straightforward; some are easy going in their personality; some are funny, excited; and so on. You get my drift?

Stay true to your nature when you do the offer. Do not change your personality or change your style. Stay true to you and modify the structure to your way of being. If you just gave a seminar that was hilarious the entire way through, make the sales part is just as funny. If you are a bulldog when it comes to delivering a seminar, be the bulldog when you are making an offer.

If you find that your participants are mentally checking out when you start with your sale, or even worse they are leaving the room, I would like to let you know that there are usually two reasons for this.

When people ask: What do you do? I say: Whatever it takes.
—unknown author

Hazard One—You Changed your Style of Delivery

Your voice changed: suddenly it adopted a different pitch. You become very serious, even though for the past few hours you had a blast with your participants. You start talking fast like there is no tomorrow. Some presenters have an extreme change, some moderate, some mild, but almost everyone changes. Maybe they are nervous or they do not feel confident. Maybe they think they are bad sales people.

Their entire personality changes.

Selling something is no different than teaching someone about a product or a service that you feel they should have in their lives.

The past few hours or even days you just gave awesome value to all your participants. They loved your program, they had a great time with you, and you established a trust with them in you. Why shouldn't you want to offer to them the next step in working with you or using your product?

Hazard Two—You changed your Design of Delivery

You stopped educating your participants; you stopped giving them value. Suddenly they got the signal that the seminar is over and done with, and it is time to stop listening to you or even get up and walk out of the room.

Develop your curriculum around the sales process. Stay congruent and give new knowledge, give value and keep being the great guy or girl you have been the past few hours or days. Have fun selling and have them keep coming back.

Use the template, but make it yours, not mine. It has to fit your style, your personality. It has to fit you. Keep teaching your participants and give them a ton of value even during the sales process, and I promise you, you too will have a great sales experience.

You will get the opportunity to keep working with your participants for many more seminars, and they will keep shopping with you for a long time. There are many different type of sales templates.

This one works for me, so find the one that works for you too. Experiment if necessary, but take your time, make it work and then stick with it.

Happy Sales Day!

The Ending is as Important as the Beginning

This is a short template for how to do a powerful ending at your seminar.

- Talk about the three most important topics that your participants just got from the seminar.

- Review some of the topics that went extremely well, the knowledge and the fun they had.

- Have your participants vow to take some action, commitments they might want to make towards their future success.

- Hand out a feedback sheet. Let participants know that you are always looking to improve the program and that their views and comments are important to you.

- If you can throw in one more ritual, maybe one last gift, or celebration, that is always a highlight for your participants.

- Thank your crew at that time and allow participants to show their appreciation.

- Good Bye and Thank you.

Over the past twelve years I found out that time invested is also a currency that people not always like to spend. If I want people to invest their money into purchasing my seminar I have to give them a so-called "taste sample" of me and my programs.

Some of the big, successful seminar leaders give you a two- or three-day (either free or very inexpensive) starter program. Those are the ones that are usually already very well known and established. But still, they want to offer you something for free knowing very well that at that low-cost or free seminar you will be more than happy to purchase their advanced seminars on the back end. The important part of offering a two- or three-day seminar is that they already heard from a valuable source or heard from you that this is the best show on the planet. Otherwise people won't invest their time, even if it is for free.

Some seminar leaders offer free online webinars or podcasts. Those usually do really well with online marketing geniuses. I am not one of them. (I wish I were.) And then there are the ones, and most of us started out like that (even the very successful seminar leaders of today) who give a "taste sample". That sample can be online, but it also can be a mini presentation of 30/60/90 minutes.

Most organization, churches, women's clubs, etc. love to have speakers. I mention this to my coaching clients and sometimes when I hear "I don't speak for free" I always have to scratch my head and ask "Why not?" Then I go into explaining that when I get a room full of people that are willing to listen to my presentation I know very well, that at the end I am going to walk away with a bunch of them attending my next seminar/workshop. My cash register just rang loud and clear. Don't expect organizations to pay you for your speeches, talk for free, but only, if you are allowed to sell your product at the end and only if you know that your ideal clients are sitting in the chairs at that event.

Once your ideal clients get to experience you in one of their events, the next step is to invite them to a several hour or daylong seminar that is quite reasonably priced. At that seminar they get to know you much better, and then you can sell them the 2-day or weekend seminar. The value of these events is huge, just like the 30/60/90, several hour, or one day seminar. The value must be excellent—this is why your ideal clients want to keep coming back.

At the weekend seminar you then get the opportunity to sell the weeklong seminars, coaching programs, and other seminars over and over again until your ideal clients have done all the seminars you have to offer—then go and create some more!

Template 1—The Thirty-Minute Miracle Presentation

If you got to this point in the book, you already learned everything you need to know for your presentation to have success. It will take some time to learn it all, so feel free to go back and reread the book—often. I am sure every time you scan over the book you will find new things that you overlooked before. This is not for casual reading, but a book to digest chapter by chapter. It will take time and practice to become familiar and fluid with all these tools. But I promise you one thing, these tools work. They are a proven strategy!

So, keep practicing and you will have amazing results! Here again you will find some steps and structure on how you can put together your first thirty-minute presentations. Here is an outline that will work for you.

Most beginners bring too much information and material to the table and there is no need for it. In fact, when I work with my clients we truly look at what course material is important. Many times we toss out 90% of what they want to cover in their presentations. Why? Most of that stuff is neither important nor necessary in the first presentation.

The first presentation is here for you to find out if your ideal client is sitting in front of you. How do you know? They will most likely buy your programs, if you did a great job connecting with them on a human level, if you talked about their one to three top problems and gave them an insight that you are the expert that can solve these issues effectively.

- For the welcome you take about five minutes: That includes scan, two questions, your name and the title of the seminar. Welcome the participants and thank the invitees. That will lead you right into the "what's in it for me" section. Last but not least, the "earn the right" section.

- After that you have about fifteen minutes to talk about the topic(s) and bring in a mini-exercise (hands-on), maybe even a partner share. Don't forget to seed the product you want to offer. A question and answer section might be appropriate.

- In the next ten minutes you make the offer for the participants to purchase your next product and at the same time you work on another problem that they become aware of. Make sure you let the participants know how they can profit from the upcoming seminar. Go through the price structure as you learned it, but mostly ask them to take action!

As always, I say try it out, practice it, make sure it fits your personality…but I want you to know that this is a proven formula that works! This is what I teach people in 5 days how to do.

When they've followed the instructions and this outline, their success has doubled, even tripled, and has taken them to a level that exceeded their expectations. So even if it doesn't feel comfortable in the beginning, don't shy away. Stick with it, keep going back to this basic outline and have fun with it. It does get easier over time. If you are lucky and have 45 or 60 minutes for your presentation add one more topic and take more time for the sales part. Your wallet will thank you for it! Have fun!

Master of Ceremony Introduction

Be yourself. Everyone else is already taken.
—Oscar Wilde

Sometimes you don't get the chance to introduce yourself. Nonetheless, it is still your responsibility to write your own introduction the way you want it to be and give it to the Master of Ceremonies, who will do the introduction for you. I can't tell you how many times people have messed up my intro. Not only my name, that is a given, but stuff where I was wondering why the heck would they say that about me—even though it mostly was really meant well.

Here is some input on how you can avoid bad intros:

- Write your own introduction and give it to the Master of Ceremony in plenty of time, so that you can correct your name and so that she has the chance to read it over a couple of times before actually introducing you.

- Please keep in mind that no one cares where you went to school, where you live, how many times you were married and how many kids/grandkids, etc. you have. Really, no one gives a hoot—so don't write it down.

- In the introduction you get to shine! Don't be modest about your credentials. Your audience wants to know what you have accomplished in your life. Your awards, your knowledge in your specific field, the things you do for other people and the community. Stuff you probably don't want to say about yourself. That is exactly what the Master of Ceremonies wants to convey to the audience.

- Remember that the participants are investing their time (and sometimes their money) to hear you speak. So they must be informed as to why you are the right person to educate them about this subject, at this time, and what actually gives you the right to talk about it. Why this subject, why now and most important why you!

Template 2—A "One Day" Time Table

Okay, one more bonus coming your way. I know that this one really helped me a lot when I started writing seminars for myself and for others. One of my favorite coaching subjects is to help my clients craft their first one-day seminars!

First we plan out the time line, then the segments and breaks, and then we fill the segments with value. Add stage changes, exercises, room share, sales segment and of course some fun in it too. Here is the basic time line for a successful one-day seminar:

- 9:00AM Beginning of Seminar—Welcome, Introduction and Rules
- 9:30 to 11:00AM—Segment 1
- 11:00 to 11:15AM—Break 1
- 11:15 to 12:30PM—Segment 2

- 12:30 to 2:00PM—Working Lunch
- 2:00 to 3:15PM—Segment 3
- 3:15 to 3:30PM—Break 2
- 3:30 to 4:00PM—Sales Segment
- 4:00 to 4:30PM—Segment 4
- 4:30 to 5:00PM—Closing of Seminar

Yes, it is that easy. Of course, you can add more segments to spread over dinner and evening into the night. But this is the basic template for how to create a one-day seminar.

Your clients want more? No problem—just repeat! You can also add all kinds of exercises, games, coaching time, meditation, whatever your heart desires. This formula is unlimited—so don't limit yourself. Be creative with your content, time and how much fun you can have with it. Keep reading and you also will find the 10 Easy Steps for a Success Path in your Seminar Business. Again, look at the big trainers out there...doesn't all of this look familiar? If they can have success with it—so can you! If you want to create a weekend seminar or a weeklong seminar, just repeat the day template several times.

Now you not only know how to put together a presentation, workshop, day or weeklong seminar, you also know how to sell your products and your services effectively.

I would like to personally invite you to try out the things that you learned from this book. I am sure some of it is already old hat for you, but I am also convinced that you found a few new tricks.

The truth is you actually don't really have to believe me at all. Why? Because it is my experience? Sure, I have visited many seminars, read many books, and talked to many other colleges before putting this book together. But ultimately I tried it out, before I put ink on paper (typed it in my computer). I too struggled in the beginning, but now it has become pure fun, and I love helping others to get on stage themselves, so they too can live their dreams of being a trainer, seminar leader or workshop leader; or just simply sell their products. I hope that our paths will cross one day if they haven't already. And from the bottom of my heart I wish you the most success that there is in life—much love, joy and happiness!

A Big Thank You

Jason, Austin and Becca, Tara and Tyler...
...you are the reasons I believe.

Karin Hollerbach, PhD—for your friendship and without you this book would still be on my laptop, waiting.

Thank you to my test readers: Ann O'Connell, Anita and Brad Wiggins, Cynthia Gstettenbauer, Irmgard Kravogel, Sabine Hankiewicz, Shana Hollinger—you guys are always there for me and I am so grateful for having you be part of my life.

Chloe—you are my secret weapon to happiness.

These are people (in alphabetical order and not in order of importance) I have learned from, taken note of, and admired for their success in the seminar world:

Brendon Burchard—https://brendon.com—Your enthusiasm on stage and in life is addicting and your eagerness to help people inspiring.

Byron Katie—http://thework.com—Your gentleness and the love you radiate is my biggest wish and my greatest challenge to conquer in this lifetime.

Callan Rush—http://www.callanrush.com—Magnetize your Audience—It all started with you, when we did an all-nighter, so I was able to face my audience with confidence.

Gail Kingsbury—http://gailkingsbury.com—Your family and friends always come first , and inside of this kind creature roars the lion of a business woman with a vision to heal the world.

Jack Canfield—http://jackcanfield.com—A class act of integrity and wisdom. I can learn from you over and over and over again.

Landmark Education—https://www.landmarkworldwide.com—In the year 2000 my journey started with entering the doors of the Forum. I never looked back.

Margo Majdi—https://www.mittraining.com—In your trainings you open people's hearts and minds that you hold safely.

T. Harv Eker—https://www.harveker.com—You are the Master of our trade. You gave me no choice—but to learn from you.

John L. Macchia—We both laugh in the face of a good challenge!

ENCORE—Big Screw-Ups you can Make as a Seminar Leader

YOUR PROGRAM HAS no real value. If you can't solve a real problem for people right now, then find one.

The problem has to be real for your participants, not just in your head. It isn't good enough to just want to help people "live the life of their dreams," "empower them" or I constantly hear "help them get to the next level."

Next level of what? More pain? More problems? No, become their problem solver and you've got a great seminar/product for sale.

Your program is not specific enough. You talk about all kinds of stuff, but you are not focused on what is really important for your participants. Where is the true pain and how can you help them solve it? The bigger the pain that they want to have solved, the bigger the value when you solve it for them.

Your program has too much information. Please don't confuse information with value. My head is spinning with all the stuff seminar leaders put in their presentations.

Information overload.

My little brain cannot digest it all at once. You are trying to teach me too much stuff in too short of a time. As if I would run away if you took the time to really help me solve one problem at a time.

You are unclear about what you are teaching or selling. You have too many offers and are trying to sell too much at one time. It doesn't work. Get clear about what you are offering, and get clear about your message. Tailor the message to your specific participants and be clear about what specific problem you are solving for them.

Then stick to it.

You have a great program, but don't know how to sell the next one. Go back a few pages, find your selling style and practice, practice, practice your sale, and then please make me an offer. A seminar without a sale does not help me. I just started to trust you, I had fun with you, I learned a lot and you solved some of my problems/ issues. I want more. So give it to me!

You are not being congruent with your programs. They have to build on top of each other and harmonize with each other, so no matter what seminar I am taking from you, I can take another one. Again, and again, and again. Allow me to grow in your seminars.

Your marketing efforts to fill your programs are not good enough to fill the room. You have a great message, know how to solve problems and heal the pain of your participants. But your marketing can't reach them. You could be the best in what you do, but if no one knows about you, then you are the best kept secret— and what good is that?

You are operating by the seat of your pants. No plan, no next step. Just as it comes. Well it won't come, and you won't succeed. "First you plan your work, and then you work your plan."

You don't network with other seminar leaders or other experts that could help you speak on their stages. On your own, you don't know enough people to bring your message to the masses. Use other experts to help you share your intentions and your message to the world.

If you don't know how to get people to your seminar room, you will have empty chairs and an empty bank account. I heard that at the Magnetize your Audience seminar with Callan Rush. You need to know how to fill your room. Take her seminar!

You are doing everything yourself. I stopped that a long time ago. First it is way too much work, and second it is no fun at all.

Share the workload as well as your success with others.

Allow people to contribute to your life, and you contribute to theirs.

Many hands are better than one!

Your work is going to fill a large part of your life, and the only way to be truly satisfied is to do what you believe is great work. And the only way to do great work is to love what you do. If you haven't found it yet, keep looking. Don't settle. As with all matters from the heart, you'll know when you find it.
—Steve Jobs

About the Author

MARGIT E. MACCHIA, born in a small village in Austria, most of her childhood dreamed on being on stage. Never did she think that forty years later, she actually would lead trainings and workshops to help people make their business dreams come true, creating and leading their own seminars, workshops, and trainings.

After years of working for world-class seminar leaders, participating and volunteering hundreds of hours in their workshops, being part of her education, she finally graduated to her own workshops and trainings. She also coaches and accompanies world-class trainer to the top of their careers.

In her spare-time, Margit took opportunities to lead fundraising teams for schools, churches and private organizations. She also served and worked with Non-profit organizations like *Circle of Hope*, *Kids Helping Kids*, *Michael Hoefflin Foundation*, *Make a Wish Foundation*, *Chess for Kids* and the *Canyon Theatre Guild*.

Helping others was, and always will be, the purpose of her life's journey. Currently she is coaching clients from all around the world. Her biggest passion is to write and teach others how to write their own seminars, workshops and trainings.

The Trainer's Toolbox is a collection of her work and experience, while having fun!

Services Available

Margit E. Macchia speaks to organizations to the U.S. and German markets.

For further information please contact her at:

Proventus, LLC
7185 Pine Street
Las Vegas, NV 89120

...or email at coachmargit@gmail.com

...or call (661) 992-2161

www.ingramcontent.com/pod-product-compliance
Lightning Source LLC
Chambersburg PA
CBHW021341090426
42742CB00008B/694